LIBERATION THEOLOGY

Human Hope Confronts Christian History and American Power

ROSEMARY RUETHER

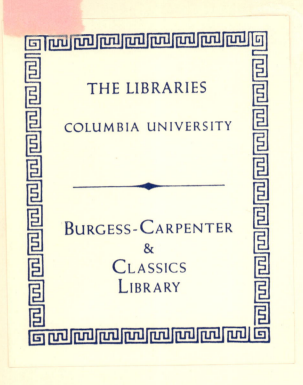

LIBERATION THEOLOGY

LIBERATION THEOLOGY

Human Hope Confronts Christian History and American Power

ROSEMARY RADFORD RUETHER

PAULIST PRESS
New York / Paramus / Toronto

Acknowledgments

Much of the material in this volume was published previously in substantially the present form.

Chapter Two appeared in *Dialog,* vol. 10 (Summer, 1971), pp. 193-200.

Chapter Three appeared in *Christian Century* (April 7, 1971), p. 425ff.

Chapter Four is a revised form of an article that appeared in *Commonweal* (1972).

Chapter Five is a revised version of an article that appeared in *Studies in Religion/Sciences Religieuses: Revue Canadienne* vol. II, no. 1 (Spring, 1972).

Chapter Six appeared in *Christianity and Crisis* (April 17, 1972), pp. 91-94.

Chapter Eight appeared in *Christianity and Crisis,* vol. 31, no. 21 (Dec. 13, 1971), pp. 267-273.

Chapter Ten appeared in the *Ecumenist,* vol. 9, no. 4 (May/June, 1971), pp. 52-57.

Chapter Eleven brings together in revised form material published in two articles: "The White Liberal in the Mother Country," *Commonweal* (Nov. 6, 1970), pp. 142-145, and "A Radical Liberal in the Streets of Washington," *Christianity and Crisis,* vol. 31, no. 12 (July 12, 1971), pp. 144-146.

Chapters Two and Ten were originally given as part of a lecture series on Social Radicalism and the Radical Church Tradition at Bethany Theological Seminary (Church of the Brethren), November, 1970, and printed in the Bethany Seminary Colloquium.

The excerpt from Frantz Fanon's *Toward the African Revolution* is reprinted by permission of Monthly Review Press. First published in France under the title of *Pour la Revolution Africaine* © 1964 by François Maspero. English translation © 1967 by Monthly Review Press. All rights reserved.

Contents

v

LIBERATION THEOLOGY

Chapter 1

The Foundations for
a Theology of Liberation

This book brings together essays, some previously published, some unpublished, which attempt to glimpse the question of human liberation today from a variety of perspectives. The essays will focus on the question of human liberation primarily from the situation of the "oppressor-oppressed" relationship, as this applies to Christian anti-Semitism, racism, sexism and colonialism. It will also ask questions of the resources of the Christian tradition to provide symbols for the liberation of peoples whom the very culture created in the name of Christianity has helped to oppress. It will be looking to what transformations need to take place to transform Christianity from a Constantinian to a prophetic religion; from an ideology of the oppressor to a gospel of liberation for the oppressed, and through the oppressed, for the oppressor as well. Many other crucial problems for human liberation will thereby be left largely untouched. The thorough knowledge of economics in its international development, and the social and economic effects of technology are also crucial for an understanding of the prospects of human liberation today. The integration of the psychological and the social sciences is essential also to overcome that impasse between Marx and Freud which has impeded the modern self-reflection on its own situation. But such a fuller integration of the sciences necessary for the fullest reflection on the question of human liberation today cannot be done by a single scholar. It waits upon a multi-disciplinary teamwork that can integrate the many sources of data and the types of reflection and symbolization around the core of theological reflection. Only with such a multi-disciplinary integration of human sciences can we begin to speak of the basis for a theology of liberation adequate to the present human situation.

Such a statement as the above, of course, suggests that the scope and nature of theology are going through a striking transformation in the present era. It is beginning to find its place as the mode of reflection that mediates between the existence and the transcendent horizon of human life. Theology is losing its confinement as an exclusively ecclesiastical science, but only because it is finding its place in a reintegrated view of the human community. It is losing its place as the science of a particular ecclesiastical tradition or even of a single historical faith, such as Christianity, but only because it is beginning to glimpse its place as the horizon of a human history that is truly catholic. It is losing its place as a science confined to the sacral or the "religious" sphere, but only because it is finding its place within the totality of human activities and the arts and sciences that reflect on and create these activities.

Theologians today are becoming generalists to an extent scarcely dreamed of, even in the high Middle Ages, when theology reigned as the queen of arts and sciences in the medieval university. In the best religion departments in universities today we find students taking courses in "religion," because this is becoming the one place where questions of ultimate meaning and value, relative to all the human sciences, can be asked. Theologians today must be even more willing to dissolve the traditional perimeters of their "field," its sources and content, in order to rise to the task of sketching the horizon of human liberation in its fully redemptive context. If theology is really to speak meaningfully about the mediating point between the "is" and the "ought" of human life, then it takes as its base the entire human project, in the histories of the cultures of many peoples and in the diverse sciences of human activities, and finds in this total spectrum the framework for asking the ultimate questions about the *humanum;* its fall and its redemption.

The theologian must, at least by intention, become the generalist *par excellence,* seeing as his context and data the whole range of human sciences and the whole history of human cultures of self-symbolization. But he does this not to create a "universal science," but rather to address to the human situation in its existence "up 'til now" a particular set of questions. It is this set of questions, *in relationship to* human history and existence, that defines what theology is as distinct from sciences which are "merely descriptive." The theological questions have to do with the fundamental tension points between the "is" and the "ought" of human life. They rise from the fundamental contradiction between man's existence and his essence; between man's existence and his aspirational horizon of meaning and value. Out of this tension and contradiction arise the fundamental theological questions about man's "nature," his "origin" and his "goal"; how man can transform himself in his personal and social history and what "power" and from whence mediates between this transcendent "nature," "ground" and "goal," and his "fallen" reality. These questions can be readily recognized by traditionally-trained Christian theologians as the basic credal doctrines of God, man, creation and fall, sin and redemption, Christology and eschatology. But these doctrines are no longer taken so much as answers than as ways of formulating the questions. These questions no longer find answers in once and for all events of a particular sacred history, so much as these histories themselves provide particular paradigmatic experiences used by different cultures for symbolizing these questions. Finally, these questions are no longer "about" a particular aspect of man called "religious," confined to an ecclesiastical sphere and a sacred history, and find their place within the human community and its history. However, this dissolving of the sacral sphere into that of the *humanum* does not make this a "secular theology" either. If the "sacral," as an interpretation of the sphere of theology, abstracted the transcendent horizon of human life into a special "religious" world where it lost its real human context, so the "secular" was merely the reverse of this one-sidedness, in the removal of a transcendent dimension of human life and the reduction of life to the purely immanent and one-dimensional. "Secularism," in this sense, gave rise to an ideological viewpoint and ideological sciences, because they ratified an oppressive *status quo* as the "norm" of truth, and denied the existence of a transcendent horizon of life whereby this oppressive *status quo* could be judged and transcended. Today we find a criticism of this secularist viewpoint among those who reflect on a variety of human activities. With the formation of an *avante garde* in various fields; i.e., "radical historians," "radical sociologists," "radical psychiatrists," "radical educators," "radical economists," and even "radical technologists," we are beginning to see the sciences of all human activities starting to recover a sense of their own transcendent horizon and the need to pose prophetic and iconoclastic questions about the normative status of the *status quo*. Theology today then integrates itself with this transcendent and prophetic horizon of all the sciences and modes of reflection upon human existence.

This reconstruction of the universal framework, nature and sources of theological reflection does not ignore, however, the reality of particular religious traditions. Indeed, we are far from the place that could do more than hint at this framework. Theology does not possess such an integrated consciousness, comparable to the range of human histories and human activities, within which to ask its questions. Rather it is itself a part of a process of creating this fuller consciousness. It is the task of theologians to situate the definition of theology within the total *humanum*. But this does not do away with the task of digging deeply into the history and development of their particular traditions, in order to discover how the symbolism of this tradition arose and developed out of primary revelatory experience. They must also chart the course of development whereby the full dynamic of this symbolism became aborted of its promise, allowing the transforming horizon of human existence to be deformed into a "wall" of falsifying dualisms between contrary "worlds" and "substances." Theology was thus deprived of its real content. Theologians in various traditions of human self-symbolization, as they struggle to overcome these falsifying dualisms in their own faiths, begin to find the points of convergence with each other, and to both glimpse and create a new consciousness for a new humanity. These essays are a part of that process within the Christian and specifically the Roman Catholic tradition. While assuming the universal context which has been spelled out above as the datum for asking theological questions, these essays will also grapple constantly with Catholic Christian doctrinal and institutional history, especially in its classical period in the Church Fathers, in order to find out where and how the insights of this tradition lapsed into falsifying dualisms and lost their prophetic dynamic. Yet these essays will also presume that this history and the very process of asking such questions of this history make it a fertile ground for the reconstruction of this symbolism in its prophetic dynamic for today. Such a mediation between past and present assumes that the past is essential for our understanding of what we can be in the light of what we have been. But it also assumes that the period of classical orthodox Christianity, and indeed classical religion generally, is in a process of being transcended today.

We might speak of the religious history of mankind as falling into three large time periods. The first period was that of tribal religion. In tribal religion the gods were integrated into the primal, and especially the agricultural rhythms of human life. Man and gods, society and nature, individual and community formed one community of life and death. This religion spoke for "man" and the "universe," but the limits of its horizon for this humanity and universe were the tribal identity and its home territory. The second period, that of classical religion, arose roughly about the sixth century B.C., with Zoroastrianism and Platonism, and the Jewish prophets, and extended through the formation of classical Christianity,

Talmudic Judaism and Islam. This new religious development; what is sometimes called the "axial period," attempted to expand its view of man and the universe to cover a truer universalism, but succeeded culturally only in expanding to cover the limits of a syncretistic empire such as that embraced in the Greco-Roman and Iranian worlds in the period of classical antiquity. The "universalism" of Christianity, for example, remained largely confined to those of Greco-Roman cultural background. Thus the universalism of these new religions remained partially ideological; a tribalism writ large, even though they were reaching for a new cosmopolitan view of the *humanum*. The peoples of alternative cultural basins were excluded from its definition of salvation and/or made dependent on adopting its own religious symbolism. But, even more important, classical religions were born through a breakdown of the unities of tribal culture and the appearing of a way of formulating a "religious dimension" of life which split reality into distinct polarities; the sacred and the secular; the individual and the community; the soul and the body; the material and the spiritual; "this world" and the transcendent world "to come" or "above." It is this classical period of religious consciousness which is breaking down today, with the breakdown of the classical civilizations of all the great basins of culture.

The present crisis in religion, therefore, is not one that can be solved by a "reformation" based on the "purification" of these traditions within their essential limitations. Rather we must recognize that the period when the formulations of classical religion answered to the stage of consciousness of human development is now mysteriously, but evidently, crumbling around and within us. We are entering into the age of "no religion at all" (to quote the famous phrase from Bonhoeffer's *Letters and Papers from Prison*), at least as religion was defined during the period of classical cultures. The very definition of "religion," as this was understood within the dualistic framework of classical religion and its institutions, is breaking down with the superceding of this stage of human perception of reality. We seem to be emerging into a new stage of consciousness where what was previously called "religion," must find its place, not as a separate "sacred sphere," but as the trans-forming horizon of human existence. We have entered the era of the "demise of heaven" and the death of the "spiritual," and of the God who was defined in terms of one side of these dualisms. We are entering an era wherein man can affirm his sense of having deeper roots and higher horizons than those of the immediate *status quo* only by pouring back the tradi-tional polarities into dynamic unities; dynamic unities between the historical and the transcendent; the spiritual and the somat-ic; the holy and the worldly. This does not mean that no resources exist for this new perspective within classical Chris-tianity and even within the unities of tribal religion, which were, in various aspects, transmitted through the medium of classical religion or which have been revived through contem-porary students of primitive religion. But these must go through a profound transformation to a new integration that as much transcends the spiritualism and other-worldliness of classical Christianity, as this transcended the crude unities of ancient Ba'alism. Christianity, for example, inherited from its syncre-tism of Jewish apocalypticism and hellenistic gnosticism, a series of polarities which now stand as basic barriers to not only a theology of liberation, but the *praxis* of liberation as well. Theologies of hope or revolution or theologies of in-wardness and mystical self-discovery will not succeed in doing more than reproducing much of what has been the limitations and even the sicknesses of classical Christianity, unless these dualisms are critically analyzed and located in a more holistic perspective. It is the purpose of the remaining pages of this essay to analyze these dualisms and their contribution to the dilemma of human self-bondage under a series of crucial categories. It is hoped thereby to sketch out the critical dimen-sions of a theology of liberation.

The Individual and the Collective

The Biblical prophetic view, inheriting some of the unities of tribal religion, did not pull apart the individual from the community and the cosmos, but held these together within a holistic view of creation and its future promise of redemption. In Israel there was a development from tribal collectivism to a greater awareness of the participation and responsibility of the individual within the promise of the group, to be sure. But, even in St. Paul, the personal movement of conversion and reconciliation with God, cannot be separated from his ingathering into the community of reconciliation and promise, for these are two sides of one and the same thing. By the same token it is clear that, for St. Paul, the state of sin, alienation and brokenness between man and God, does not result simply in individual "bad acts" but stands within a corporate structure of alienation and oppression which has raised up a social and cosmic "anti-creation." This is what St. Paul calls "the Powers and Principalities" or the "Elementary Principles of the Universe." The individualistic concept of sin ignores this social-cosmic dimension of evil. A concentration on individualistic repentance has led, in Christianity, to a petty and privatistic concept of sin which involves the person in obsessive compunction about individual (mostly sexual) immorality, while having no ethical handle at all on the great structures of evil which we raise up corporately to blot out the face of God's good creation. In our "private confession" we have, in effect, involved people in a process of kneeling down to examine a speck of dirt on the floor while remaining oblivious to the monsters which are towering over their backs. Indeed privatistic religion systematically excludes attention to these corporate and social monsters by excluding them from their very definition of sin and repentance in a "religious" framework; i.e., "politics has nothing to do with religion."

A prophetic sense of sin might indeed acknowledge that sin begins in the personal *"cor curvum in se,"* but its expression is corporate, social and even cosmic. Sin builds up a corporate structure of alienation and oppression which man, individually, cannot overcome, because he has fallen victim to his own evil creations as the very social fabric of his "world." This corporate structure of sin distorts the character of man in community and in creation so fundamentally that it can be visualized as a false "world"; an anti-society and anti-cosmos where man finds himself entrapped and alienated from his "true home," and he cries out for a transcendent liberation which will overcome "this world" and bring him back to his "original home in paradise." But "this world" is *not* God's creation, and so the solution to this dilemma is not a flight from creation to "heaven," but an overthrowing of this false world which has been created out of man's self-alienation, and a restoration of the world to its proper destiny as "the place where God's will is done on earth, as it is in heaven."

Nature and Grace

Liberation begins in grace and moves from this foundation in grace to the possibility of self-judgment and repentance. Liberation is not a fruit or reward of repentance, so much as it is the ground and possibility of repentance. Liberation begins in a gratuitous mystery of freedom that happens within our situation, yet beyond the capacities of the alienated situation iself. It is experienced as a free gift "from above." It is only in that gratuitous and transcendent mystery of freedom, that dawns upon us without our "deserving" it, and before we have articulated our need for it, that we find ourselves able to enter into this articulation and transformation. Repentance then is simply the power to disaffiliate our identity from the false and oppressive power systems of fallen reality. But the gift of liberation, although alien and transcendent to the situation of sin, is not alien to "our natures," but springs from the same "ground" as man's original foundation. So it is not properly seen as "supernatural," but as a restoration of man to his true self, and a reintegration of creation with its true destiny as "God's Kingdom."

Because Christianity adopted in its early formation a gnosticizing separation of redemption from creation, it has created a false dilemma of "nature and grace" which was foreign to the Hebraic perspective. (It has also projected upon Judaism the negative side of this dichotomy by defining its view of salvation as "carnal" and "materialistic." Thus Christian anti-Semitism

and Christian gnosticism are two sides of a similar distortion.)
Today we must strive for a perspective on liberation that
overcomes these dichotomies. We must recognize that the movement of revolt against false and oppressive worlds of "Powers
and Principalities" is integral to the renewal of the world
whereby creation and bodily existence become the vehicle and
theophany of God's transcendent appearing; i.e., creation becomes the place for the appearance of God's *Shechinah*. It is
around such an interpretation of God's *Shechinah* that Christianity might be able to reestablish with Judaism some new
dialogue about the meaning of "incarnation." God's presence
does not appear just in one time and place "once for all," but
wherever reconciliation is established and man glimpses his
unity and the unity of the world with its transcendent foundation and meaning. A religious culture may pick out a particular
place where this appearing is seen "normatively"; i.e., Jesus or
the Torah or Buddha, but this doctrine of "incarnation" is not
just "about" this one place or person, but this one place or
person operates as a norm for discerning the nature of this
"presence" wherever it happens.

The Oppressor and the Oppressed as a Model
for Liberation Theology

Recent theologies of liberation have stressed the role of the
"oppressed community" as the primary locus of the power for
repentance and judgment. God's liberation is seen as coming
first to the "poor." God liberates the slaves from the oppressive
system of power, symbolized by Egypt. God comes to overturn
the oppressive reign of imperial power symbolized by Babylon
(Rome; Amerika).

It is true that such a dualism of the "children of light" and
the "children of darkness" can be extracted from prophetic
thinking. However, this dualism, in its polarized form, appears
primarily in the literature of apocalypticism. The thinking of
the prophets addressed Israel as, simultaneously, the community of Promise and the community which must repent and be

judged. Liberation, therefore, cannot be divorced from a sense of self-judgment and an identification with the community which is judged. It cannot be merely a movement of revolt against and judgment of an "alien community" for which one takes no responsibility. The paranoid projection of all evil upon the "nations," whereby Israel is seen simply as the "suffering saints," distorts this prophetic dialectic. Indeed such a total polarization is not found even in the apocalyptic writings, which never fail to address Israel itself as the one which must repent and be judged and return to obedience. Christianity inherited, through apocalyptic sectarian Judaism (further accentuated by the break between the sectarian apocalyptic community and ethnic Israel), the possibility of a one-sided distortion of the prophetic dialectic that would locate one community as the "oppressed saints," and the heirs of the Promise, while projecting upon the oppressors (Rome) and the rejectors (ethnic Israel) all evil and condemnation.

Such a viewpoint which judges "God's people" and "God's enemy" from the standpoint of the oppressed and the oppressors has, nevertheless, a real theological validity to it. Contextually, this historical situation does indeed become the primary place of prophetic discernment. Marxist systems, Black theology and Latin American theologies of liberation, constructed on this apocalyptic sectarian model, can carry a process of judgment and liberation a considerable distance. But, at a certain point, this model for the theology of liberation begins to reveal the limitations and disabilities inherent in its inadequate foundations.

There is a sense in which those who are primarily the victims of an oppressive system are also those who can most readily disaffiliate their identities with it, for they have the least stake in its perpetuation. In their revolt against it, they can thus become the prophetic community, which witnesses against the false empire of the "beast" and points to "God's Kingdom." But, in their very situation as victims, they have also been distorted in their inward being in a way that does not immediately make them realized models of redeemed humanity; i.e., the victims are not "saints." They have a very considerable task of inward liberation to do. They have been victimized by their powerlessness, their fear and their translation of these into an internal appropriation of subservient and menial roles. They have internalized the negative image projected upon them by the dominant society. They cower before the masters, but are also filled with a self-contempt which makes them self-destructive and fratricidal toward their fellows within the oppressed community. Typically the oppressed turn their frustration inward, destroying themselves and each other, not the masters.

Liberation for the oppressed thus is experienced as a veritable resurrection of the self. Liberation is a violent exorcism of the demons of self-hatred and self-destruction which have possessed them and the resurrection of autonomy and self-esteem, as well as the discovery of a new power and possibility of community with their own brothers and sisters in suffering. Anger and pride, two qualities viewed negatively in traditional Christian spirituality, are the vital "virtues" in the salvation of the oppressed community. Through anger and pride the oppressed community receives the power to transcend self-hatred and recover a sense of integral personhood. Anger, here, is felt as the power to revolt against and judge a system of oppression to which one was formerly a powerless and buried victim. Pride is experienced as the recovery of that authentic humanity and good created nature "upon which God looked in the beginning and, behold, it was very good." Anger and pride thus stand initially within the context of a prophetic dialectic of judgment and the renewal of creation.

However, at that point where all evil is merely projected upon an alien community, so that judgment is seen merely as rejection of that "other" group of persons, and salvation simply as self-affirmation, *per se,* (without regard to a normative view of humanity), then what is valid in this initial perception is quickly distorted. The leaders of the oppressed community are not incorrect when they recognize that they have, as their primary responsibility, the leading of their own people through a process of self-exorcism and renewed humanity. So there is a sense where it is true that they "do not have the time" to be worried about the humanization of the oppressor. Yet they must also keep somewhere in the back of their minds the idea that the dehumanization of the oppressor is really their primary problem, to which their own dehumanization is related primarily in a relationship of effect to cause. Therefore, to the extent that they are not at all concerned about maintaining an authentic prophetic address to the oppressors; to the extent that they repudiate them as persons as well as the beneficiaries of false power, and conceive of liberation as a mere reversal of this relationship; a rejection of their false situation of power in order to transfer this same kind of power to themselves, they both abort their possibilities as a liberating force for the oppressors, and, ultimately, derail their own power to liberate themselves. Quite simply, what this means is that one cannot dehumanize the oppressors without ultimately dehumanizing oneself, and aborting the possibilities of the liberation movement into an exchange of roles of oppressor and oppressed. By projecting all evil upon the oppressors and regarding their own oppressed condition as a stance of "instant righteousness," they forfeit finally their own capacity for self-criticism. Their revolt, then, if successful, tends to rush forward to murder and self-aggrandizement, and the institution of a new regime where all internal self-criticism is squelched. Seven demons return to occupy the house from which the original demon has been driven, and the last state of that place is worse than the first. Such has been the tendency of modern revolutionary movements patterned on the apocalyptic, sectarian concept.

The oppressor community, of course, has a similar problem in finding who it is and what it should do in relationship to the judgment and revolt of the oppressed. The first tendency of the oppressors is, of course, to respond to the liberation movement simply by projecting upon it the negative side of their own self-righteousness. Since they have already identified their own false power with the "Kingdom of Righteousness," their initial tendency is simply to identify those in revolt against this power as the "evil ones" who are ever at work to undermine the security of "God's Elect." Within this paranoid framework, each side merely sees itself as the "saints," and the others as the "beast," and no authentic communication takes place. This paranoid view, by the way, is not merely true of traditional clerical and sacral societies, such as Christendom of the European *ancien regime*. It is equally true of revolutionary societies, which have likewise been founded upon the appropriation of messianic self-imagery, such as the USSR and the USA. These modern revolutionary societies have virtually reestablished the traditional problem of Constantinian societies, although it is the opinion of this author that the USSR has a deeper problem since it passed directly from Byzantine Caesaro-papism to Marxist sectarian apocalypticism, as its political identity, without having assimilated the fruits of liberalism that could provide a theory and an institutional base for on-going self-criticism and self-correction.

Yet there are also elements in the dominant society that *are* ready to respond sympathetically to the revolt of the oppressed and to make this revolt the occasion for their own self-judgment. It is this prophetic element in the dominant society, what is usually seen as the "alienated intelligentsia," that has been, typically, the crucial mediating force for translating the protest of the oppressed into an opportunity for repentance in the dominant society. But this mediating role is also fraught with dangers and possibilities of self-delusion. The vitality of this mediating role becomes aborted when this "alienated intelligentsia" becomes concerned primarily with its own self-purification through disaffiliation with its own class, race or nation; when it seeks primarily a parasitic identification with the oppressed, who are viewed, idealistically, as the "suffering saviors," who can do no wrong or in whom all is to be excused. The prophet in the dominant society, thus becomes involved in an endless movement of self-hatred and a utopian quest for identification with and acceptance by the victims, making it impossible for him to see either side of the social equation as it really is.

Instinctively the victimized community rejects such a person, no matter how vehement his repudiation of his own people, because they sense that, in seeking to identify with them, he is taking over a leadership role which they need to learn to do for themselves. From his very social background he brings to them so much knowledge, in the way of self-confidence, expertise and familiarity with power, that he easily drowns their own feeble attempts to learn these things for themselves. Thus he interferes with their own self-discovery. Moreover, the alienated oppressor can never disaffiliate himself enough from his own society, as long as it continues in power and he automatically remains the beneficiary of that fact, to be seen by the oppressed as anything other than an extension of that fact of power over their lives in a novel form. Their own responses to the alienated oppressor who seeks to "help" them are doubtless very confused. This confusion reflects their own lack of inward liberation that makes it impossible for them to see him as other than a continuing symbol of oppression. This reflects the fact that they have not yet broken the hold of this power over their lives, and so they cannot deal with him as simply a "person" or an "exception to the rule," but react to him as a symbol of that power despite his protestations to the contrary. Yet they also discern, in a confused but valid way, that in merely adopting the echo of their own sectarian paranoia, in merely repudiating his own people and seeking identification with them, the alienated oppressor is also aborting the role of mediatorship to his own community, which is the only role in which he can be useful to them. In other words, they do not need him primarily to join what they are doing, but to play a complementary role in relation to that struggle for self-determination, by helping to get his own community off their backs so they can have a place in which to breathe. In seeking primarily to join their struggle and to move away from contact with his own people, he fails to play this vital mediating role which he alone can do for them and which they cannot do for themselves, short of successful violence.

Only when protest and response remain in dialogue in such a way that the society which is condemned is also addressed as a community which has fallen away from its own authentic promise, can there be a liberation without ultimate violence; a liberation that can end in reconciliation and new brotherhood. This cannot easily be proclaimed as a possibility before the conditions for its realization have begun to appear. It can happen only on the other side of "Black power" and

"Black pride" in the black community and repentance and surrender of unjust power on the part of the white community. This hope for a new community is aborted when the black prophet refuses to have any part with liberating the oppressor as a part of his own self-liberation. It is also aborted when the white prophet seeks merely self-exculpating identification with the victims, rather than remaining in repentant and suffering identification with his own people, until he can translate this judgment to them as their own self-judgment. This was the vision of Martin Luther King. King never forgot to address Amerika, the oppressor, as also the land of promise for black man and white man alike. This vision, declared obsolete, when King was murdered, was not so much over and done with as it represented a proleptic reaching for a prophetic wholeness, for which neither black Americans nor white Americans were ready at that time. King's vision pointed to a Black ideology beyond black racism, and beyond white paternalism or white self-exculpation, to the only validly prophetic way of doing an American theology. All theologies of liberation, whether done in a black or a feminist or a Third World perspective, will be abortive of the liberation they seek, unless they finally go beyond the apocalyptic, sectarian model of the oppressor and the oppressed. The oppressed must rise to a perspective that affirms a universal humanity as the ground of their own self-identity, and also to a power for self-criticism. The alienated oppressor must learn what it means to be truly responsible for whom and what he is.

Body-Soul and Subject-Object Dualism as the Model of Oppression

Apocalyptic dualism, interpreted as gnostic body-soul dualism, gave to classical Christianity a dualistic mode of moral, epistemological and ontological perception. Such a dualistic mode of perception of reality not only impedes a holistic theology of liberation, but it is also substantially responsible for constructing the very world of alienation from which we seek liberation. We can analyze this alienation as operating on three levels: (1) alienation from oneself; one's own body; (2) alienation from one's fellow person in the "alien" community; (3) alienation from the "world"; from the visible earth and sky.

Western epistemology and spirituality were modeled on this self-alienated view of reality. Classical Christian spirituality read sin through the eyes of gnostic body-hatred. Salvation was interpreted as coming about through the repression of the body; repression of all sensual appetites and feelings and the flight to an inward, transcendent, spiritual self. Eating, sleeping, even bathing; the delights of ear and eye; and most of all, sexual pleasure, as the most intense bodily feeling, were the veritable "seat of the devil." This constituted, literally, a death ethic. Salvation is achieved by life-long "mortification," culminating in death; the "separation of the soul from the body." Christianity, despite its struggle to correct the gnostic view of creation as a fall, ended in preserving much of this same gnostic spirituality.

However, this anti-material spirituality has by no means been entirely corrected through the modern empirical, scientific view. This is because Cartesian epistemology carried on much the same presuppositions of Platonism and couched its view of knowledge in terms of subject-object dualism. Thinking and knowing were a process whereby a non-material thinking subject reduced all around him, including his own body, to the status of an object to be mastered. Reality was split into a "non-material thinking substance" and a "non-thinking extension" or "matter." Subject-object dualism and the objectification of "outer reality" has been the basis of modern science. So, although Renaissance man repudiated one aspect of classical Christian spirituality, modern scientific man preserved an analogous bias, in a dualistic perception of outward reality as "dead matter."

This dualistic perception of reality alienates man from himself and from all perceptible reality *qua* body. The human potential movements in contemporary psychology and the ecological movement are recognitions of the way this self-alienation and world-alienation have resulted in a human being culturally divorced from the ability to integrate his own feelings with his proper self-image, and who relates to other people and to the earth in an exploitative way. Earth, air, water, plants and animals are not perceived as living "beings" who form a single community of life with himself. They are seen simply as "objects to be used." Today the human potential and the ecological movements are poised at the point where they are recognizing a common agenda and point of convergence as aspects of a single effort to reshape the way we have been taught to relate to our bodies and to the earth. But these movements have not yet found a point of convergence with the social struggle for justice and liberation of the oppressed communities of man. These two movements, therefore, are seen as unrelated or antagonistic, and oppressed people typically see the concerns of the ecological and human potential movements as the way in which the affluent drop out of the social struggle to pursue their private narcissisms.

In actuality, however, social oppression in Western culture is very closely related to the mentality that has created body-alienation and earth-exploitation. Social oppression in Western culture has operated out of a psychology which projects this same dualism of body and soul, subject and object into sociological alienation and oppression. It is not accidental that the most devastated environments, whether in Appalachia or in the ghetto, are found where poor people live. The suburbs become aware of the ecological problem, even as they become aware of the drug problem, only when it can no longer be kept invisible within the sphere of the rejected community, but begins to penetrate into the enclaves of affluence. Thus it is easy for those concerned with social justice to see the concern for ecology and reconciliation with the body as mere selfishness. But, in fact, oppression of persons and oppression of environments go together as parts of the same mentality. The rejection of a people finds its ultimate expression in the pushing of these people on to the "reservation" of ruined, waterless and unusable land. By the same token, the poor and despised in society are herded into the rotten core areas of the city where the unwillingness of the dominant society to build, except by polluting and ruining the land, is most evident.

Similarly, social alienation and exploitation have been parts of the same mentality that created this alienated view of the body and alienated view of the earth. Social oppression, in other words, has operated as a sociological projection of body-soul, subject-object dualism. Sexual or male-female dualism was the original model for this social projection of psychic dualism. Classical Christian spirituality viewed man as a "rational spirit." The male alone was said to fully possess this "human nature" in its essence. The male alone was made in the "image of God," modeled in his inward being after the intellectual *Logos* or "mind" of God (which was also the theological identity of Christ). The female was said to lack this full "image of God" in herself, and to possess it only when taken together with the male "who is her head." Likewise, women were seen as possessing no rights over their own bodies, but as standing under the tutelege and being possessed as the private property of a particular male, first their fathers, and then their husbands. Male-female dualism was seen as a social extension of subject-object dualism, so the male alone was the perceiver and the articulator of the relationship, while the woman was translated into an "object" in relation to this male perception and "use." Thus women were seen, literally, as "sexual objects," either to be used instrumentally, as a "baby-making body," or else to be shunned as the incarnation of tempting, debasing "sensuality." To be sure, Christian spirituality also affirmed the redeemability of women, but this too was read in an even redoubled way, through the basic concept of body-soul dualism, so the woman could be redeemed best by becoming the "virgin" and crushing out of herself both her bodily and also her "female" nature; even obliterating her "image," so that she no longer appeared as a "female body" before the male visual perception. This view of women and sexuality prevented Christianity from developing any positive view of the sexual relationship as an authentically inter-personal relationship. Christianity was forced into the straitjacket of a "prurient-puritan" syndrome toward relations between the sexes, from which we still suffer. Much of what is billed today as "sexual liberation" is, in fact, merely the obverse of this same "prurient-puritan" syndrome. Sex to be avoided for other than procreation is replaced by sex to be sought after as "carnal pleasure," but in either case woman is reduced to the status of a "sexual object."

Classical Christianity attributed all the intellectual virtues to the male. Woman was thereby modeled after the rejected part of the psyche. She is shallow, fickle-minded, irrational, carnal-minded, lacking all the true properties of knowing and willing and doing. Her inferiority and subjugation are rationalized by a cultural and institutional assimilation of this view that dictates the entire formation of the girl-child on this model of psychic subjugation. However, women are not the only ones to suffer from a social projection of psychic polarization. Rather we must see this sexual model as providing the basic models for all types of social oppression and its accompanying cultural appropriation and institutionalization. This same model of social projection of psychic dualism has been extended to each of the other rejected, subjugated groups in society.

Black-white relations were modeled after much the same dualism. The black man was defined originally as the "slave" in "Christian society." As slave, he was "body-object" pure and simple, to be bought, sold, used and abused as a "thing." To him likewise was attributed all the irrationality, lack of potential for initiative, thinking and willing of the subjugated psyche. The black man was seen as dangerously sensual. Although "passive," he was threateningly "passionate." He must be kept under the constant threat of brutal punishment, lest he revolt against the white male's sexual hegemony, that kept the "white woman" on a pedestal, as the model of "purity," while using the black woman as the object of debased lust. Racism was the institutionalization of this view of the black man and the black woman, modeling their entire potential for life within these limits set by white definition and use.

Such a view of the subjugated peoples as both objects of exploitation and also as beings who deserve such use by virtue of their irrational, passive, yet dangerously sensual "natures," has marked the traditional view of white males toward all "inferiors"; whether these be workers, peasants, women, blacks or colonized, especially non-white peoples. It is probably less well recognized that classical Christian anti-Semitism was also modeled on a peculiar variant of this same dualism. The Jews were defined as the people of the "letter," in contrast to Christians, who were the people of the "spirit." Judaism was defined by the Church Fathers as merely the "carnal image" of what had been fulfilled on a higher spiritual level by Christ, leaving the Jews with only an empty shell of an obsolete religion which had existed in the first place only to point beyond itself. The Jewish refusal to accept this as an appropriate judgment upon their religion was interpreted as that perverse "moral blindness" on their part which is symptomatic of their spiritual condition. The Jews were the obstinate, "grace-less" men, who could only know things "after the flesh."

This view of the Jews found its way into modern society in secular form. The Jew, forced into the role of the usurer in the Middle Ages, was associated with greed for money and material things. Thus he could be condemned by the Left as the symbol of capitalism, while simultaneously denounced by the reactionary ecclesiastical and social Right as the essence of the spirit of modern "materialism," manifest in "godless Communism." Since the Jews in the nineteenth century were emerging explosively from their long confinement to the ghetto in Christian society and numbered in their ranks some of the most successful financiers, as well as a coterie of intellectuals attracted to socialism as the movement for social justice, there was just enough evidence of prominent Jews in both camps to feed both of these kinds of bigotry. But the important thing to note here is that the stereotypes of the Left as well as the Right boil down to the same model of negativity; i.e., the Jew as the "Old Adam"; the carnal-minded, materialistic one who stands as the "enemy" of Christian spiritual aspiration and fulfilled messianism.

When we bring together the full picture of this history of aberrant spirituality, expressed in self-alienation, world-alienation, and various kinds of social alienations in sexism, anti-Semitism, racism, alienation between classes, and finally colonialist imperialism, the picture is devastating indeed. Christianity, as the bearer of this culture of aberrant spirituality and its prime mover around the world, carries a particularly deep burden of guilt for this history. The ultimate expression of this aberrant spirituality is a world divided by a technology of death, poised on the brink of annihilating the earth, while engaged in paranoid domestic repression of internal dissent. This then is the full dimensions of those "Powers and Principalities" from which we seek liberation.

The theological model for this liberation cannot be merely the apocalyptic, sectarian Armageddon, nor yet the flight of the soul from the body and the outer world to infinite inner space, for these have both become too much a part of the problem to be a credible part of the solution today. Nor can we seek liberation merely in the romantic, primitivist "body grope" of some aspects of the human potential and "encounter" movements, nor the escape from civilization to the uncultivated primal paradise of the utopian ecologists. Rather a perspective on liberation must emerge from a much more deeply integral vision which finds a new unity of opposites through transformation of values. We must revolt against and exodus from "this world"; yes, but not in infinite flight from the body, the woman and the world, but to return to that true body-self in community with our fellow persons and creation in aspiration for that "good land" of messianic blessedness which makes all things whole. We seek to become authentic co-creators with God, upon whose works God can look and declare, at last, that it is indeed "very good." We seek to become neither world-exploiters, nor world-fleers, but cultivators of the garden. The power to transcend what has become does not lead us out into an infinite flight to "heaven," but rather re-unites us with the transcendent foundation that is both the ground and the goal of what truly "is." Only that God who "will be," because he was "in the beginning" and "is," can give us the foundation and the faith to remain in this tension in fidelity, without seeking a premature resolution of tension, either in cheap grace or in cheap damnation. To remain in this tension in fidelity is to live by faith; to keep our hope for the Kingdom in the midst of inconclusiveness and our love for the brothers and sisters in the midst of brokenness. In this faith we can also begin to celebrate now.

Chapter 2

Christian Origins
and the Counter-Culture

Today we are seeing, especially in advanced technological countries such as the USA, a burgeoning movement of protest and dissent. This dissent goes far beyond the immediate dislocations of American society caused by the war in Vietnam. The dissenters see this war as part of much more intrinsic attitudes and socioeconomic structures of Western society. They would take this criticism beyond even the analysis of imperialism and exploitation proposed by traditional Marxism and question the very assumptions of scientific, technological society, for Marxism, although it attacked the social organization of production, never questioned the scientific, technological rationality itself. It is for this reason that writers such as Paul Goodman and Theodore Roszak [1] have rightly suggested that the dissenting movement in American society, despite its concentration among the young, constitutes potentially a crisis in the fundamental faith in objective, scientific reason upon which Western society has been built since the Enlightenment.

Paul Goodman in *The New Reformation* [2] stressed the religious character of the dissenting movement and compared the counter-culture to the radicals of the Reformation who raised ultimate questions about the very foundations of Christendom. I would like to take the analogy back even farther and suggest that today's cultural crisis corresponds in many ways to that cultural crisis in which Christianity itself was born. Our own time, like that of the later Roman Empire, feels an imminent doom hanging over the very construct of civilization itself.

In the Reformation period even the Radicals had Scripture as the unquestioned point of reference for criticizing society, but today all authorities are in question, and men seem to be groping around in the very rubble of civilization for half-forgotten esoterica which may furnish guidance or inspiration. In our times, as in the later Roman Empire, strange primitive shapes emerge from the dark recesses of man's historical journey, which civilized men thought they had long since left behind. Magic, astrology, demonology, shamanism, the occult, secret brotherhoods all surge into vogue, along with widespread disaffection from the official cult, politics and economic life of the dominant society. One might remember that the Renaissance and Reformation was also such a time of revival of magic and astrology and the formation of radical mystical, utopian or apocalyptic sects.

This suggests that such phenomenon arise precisely at those moments when the superstructure of a civilization is in profound crisis, and man is desperately reaching out for straws of meaning. With the rational ego and superego of the society discredited, the more deeply buried id of human society, the tribal and myth-ritual forms of the primitive past, come back to the surface from what C. G. Jung called "the collective unconscious," [3] bringing back forms and shapes which civilized man thought he had left behind, but which now appear more fundamental and basic to human survival than the fruits of the tenuously isolated island of rationality and objective consciousness. But such moments of crisis are not merely met with collective regression. There is also a utopian thrust at such times.

With the rational compromises of the prevailing system thrown into question, man is set free to dream and project radical alternatives and to envision much more total forms of salvation than historical experience has yet been able to incarnate. The time of crisis and judgment, then, also becomes a moment for the birth of far more transcendent hopes and the glimpsing of more exalted possibilities in radical contrast to the blackness of the present.

Apocalypticism and Gnosticism: Counter-Cultures of Antiquity

If one were looking for the symptoms of acute alienation in the society in which Christianity was born, and the development of counter-cultures which expressed this alienation, I would point particularly to two movements in antiquity: Jewish apocalypticism and Greco-oriental gnosticism. Christianity has traditionally appeared to be more favorable to apocalypticism than to gnosticism. Apocalypticism, after all, was the sort of sectarian Judaism out of which Christianity itself emerged. Apocalypticism forms the earliest strata of New Testament theology and continues to dominate not only such developed theological viewpoints as that of St. Paul, but also the secondary strata of the New Testament, such as James and I Peter.

The New Testament closes with one of the most dramatic and complete of all apocalyptic writings, the Revelation of John. And yet, in practice, Christianity soon curbed and then expelled apocalypticists and thereafter regarded them as fanatics and dangerous heretics, whenever they rose on the fringes of the established Church. As soon as Christianity saw itself as appropriating the higher culture of the Greco-Roman world, even claiming itself as the true representative of the higher culture, apocalypticism was no longer welcome. Indeed, in the third and fourth centuries in the Greek sectors of the Church, which was the dominant sector in theological development, there was a distinct embarrassment with the Book of Revelation and some excluded it from the canon of the New Testament.

Gnosticism, however, both within the New Testament and thereafter has regularly been regarded as the enemy. It is seen as the false, contrived and totally reprehensible way of thinking against which the orthodox Christian must resolutely set his face. However, I would argue that Christianity has roots in both these kinds of counter-cultures and in the profound alienation from the dominant world which they expressed, and Christianity ultimately prevailed because it answered for a time the radical questions which these movements raised and expressed in ancient society.

What is apocalypticism? Apocalypticism was the radicalizing of Jewish prophetism under the impact of increasingly larger and more oppressive imperial powers: Assyrian, Babylonian, Persian, Greek and Roman. Under the impact of this historical experience of oppression, God's promise of restoration to his people in a land where every man would sit under his own vine and fig tree, where all would obey the Lord from the heart and none would make war any more, these very concrete and this-worldly hopes came to be seen in an increasingly alienated or transcendent perspective, as the fulfillment of these hopes came to be seen as increasingly remote and impossible within the prevailing power structures of the world. The world as it *is* then appeared ever more alien and foreign to that which *ought to be,* not merely in a superficial, reformable sense, but right down to its root principle of existence.

The dominant form of the world came to be seen as demonic in principle, alien to man's true self, as though the very universe had fallen under the dominion of evil powers. Only some intervention from beyond which would radically overthrow the prevailing mode of the world and re-establish it on a new and entirely different basis, abolishing the reign of the evil Prince of this World, and making a new beginning with a new heaven and a new earth, could hold out any hope of salvation. This is the essential message of apocalypticism. The apocalyptic, sectarian movements within Judaism from the time of Judas Maccabees, with the Essenes, the Zealots, the Baptist preachers, including early Christianity, culminating in the rise of the Jewish people in Palestine in disastrous revolt against the Roman occupying forces in 66-70 A.D.: all this expressed a vision drawn from the apocalyptic counter-culture and acted as a resistance movement to Greco-Roman military and cultural imperialism.[4]

The vision and message of gnosticism are similar to apocalypticism. Perhaps the chief difference between the two visions is that gnosticism uses a spatial imagery of the "above" and the "below" to express its experience of alienation, judgment and transcendence, while apocalypticism uses temporal imagery about the "now" and the "time to come." This preference for spatial imagery directs gnosticism toward a more inward, mystical form of withdrawal from, and overcoming of the world, whereas the apocalyptic vision is one of assault on the prevailing world system by heavenly powers from beyond. Gnosticism expresses its protest against the world in the form of utopian or esoteric sects of ascetic, contemplative paths to salvation, while apocalypticism can lead to great upheavals of peoples, such as the messianic agitation of the first century which inspired the Jewish people to hurl itself recklessly against Roman imperial might.

Gnosticism is also born in an experience of profound alienation from the form of the existing world, but it transmutes this experience into a radically dualistic cosmology, rather than visualizing it as an historical drama of world disaster and re-creation. In gnostic thought all the old religions, all the gods and keynotes of the traditional faiths have become invalidated. They do not reveal to us the true God and the true heaven, but only evil demons of that o'er-mastering destiny which rules the prison house of the fallen universe. The divine Demiurgos of Plato, the Lord Sabaoth of the Bible; the throne of the cherubim of Ezekiel's vision, all have become demonized as fallen and alienating forces which separate rather than connect man with the true sources of his being. Even the universe itself, the starry heavens with the seven spheres of the planets and the fixed stars, which Greek cosmos piety contemplated with such rapture as the realm of the gods, has become devalued as so many encircling walls of that labyrinth which holds man in slavery to ignorance and base passion. The universe itself comes to be seen as a vast, infernal prison house of so many encircling walls trapping man in its darkest and most inaccessible core. The true heaven and the true God are far above and other than these cosmic heavens and dieties of the universe. The true Heavenly Pleroma is radically transcendent not only to all that is on earth, but all that is in the highest heaven.

Even the human constitution reflects this same predicament. Man is unknown to himself. He is like an onion, with many encircling somatic and psychic layers that bind him to ignorance of his true self and his true heavenly home. Somewhere, deeply buried within, is the spark of that transcendent home whence he originally came, but this spark of his true self is dormant, and only a transcendent call from beyond can break through the infinite walls of fate and awaken this sleeping self, draw it out of the many-layered abyss into which it has fallen and restore it to that distant and unknown heavenly realm far beyond the heavens. Such was the basic message of gnosticism.[5]

The earliest Christianity had deep roots in both these counter-cultures: revolutionary and mystical. Like them, it was born in a radical quest for a transcendent savior, but it had also experienced this savior in its midst, and so it went beyond the stance of alienation to the creation of a new cultural synthesis which was able to gather up and assimilate all that was still viable in antique culture. So compelling was its ability to absorb the old into its new gospel that finally the dominant society itself had nothing left to do but to capitulate to it (or take it over, if you will) as the mainstay of its own tottering realm. This Constantinian establishment of the Church has been the source of great debate from the time of the Reformation until now. Was this the great triumph of Christianity, or was it rather the great cop-out? [6]

There are few people today who would argue with the enthusiasm of a Bishop Eusebius that it was the great triumph. And yet, if one honestly views this development, not from the viewpoint of the discrediting of Christendom in the later Middle Ages, but rather from the viewpoint of a culture on the brink of disaster in the fourth and fifth centuries, it is hard to say that it was nothing but the great cop-out. For it is hard to imagine how either civilization or Christianity would have survived, even to the extent that they did, after the fall of the Roman Empire in the West, if Christianity had not gone beyond the antithetical stand of a gnostic or apocalyptic counter-culture and embarked on the creation of a new cultural synthesis.

Contemporary Counter-Cultures

Before we try to probe more deeply the answer to this dilemma of the relationship between Christianity and society, let us turn to the contemporary evidences of cultural crisis and alienation. Here we see a vehement protest movement against the expression of the dominant society in militarism, racism, pollution and the alienation of all the human relationships in which men conduct their daily lives. The youth especially hurl themselves against the symbols of the rejected society, but they hesitate to embark on any constructive reforms that suggest merely more effective ways of doing these same things. The culture is invalidated, not merely in its superstructure, but at its roots, and in its fundamental presuppositions.

Walter Roszak identifies this fundamental presupposition as the "myth of the objective consciousness," but I would prefer to define it, following Martin Buber,[7] as that "I-It" relationship which is the basic existential act that turns persons into things and makes all reality objectifiable and manipulatable. This is the fundamental presupposition of the scientific culture, together with all the economic, political and cultural forms which it engenders, that is under attack as the root of oppression and alienation. In revolt against this axiom of the scientific faith, the counter-culture snatches at forgotten alternatives in mysticism, magic, ecstasies, (even if drug-induced) and a personalism incarnated in new communities which seek to make all the ways in which people relate to each other—sexually, socially, economically—into expressions of love and mutual aid rather than of competition and exploitation.

The counter-culture can be said to have begun in the Civil Rights Movement of the '60s, when those who traveled to the South or to the ghettos of the North had the shocking but revealing experience of finding themselves in a counter-community over against the dominant society which, in the very process of trying to make that society fulfill its own commitments, became regarded as an alien and foreign community. Black Americans, of course, had always experienced themselves as belonging to a kind of counter-culture, so this was primarily a sharing of that experience of the black community. At the same time it came as a kind of revelatory experience to white Americans, giving them for the first time a chance to see themselves, and their own society, from "the other side." But this was not an "other side" that belonged within a pluralism recognized by the dominant society. It was precisely an unknown community, an option not taken into account at all by the dominant society. It meant sharing in a human mode of existence which did not "exist" at all in the public culture. Therefore, it became a vantage point for experiencing both alienation and transcendence. The white person, identified with the black community, stepped "outside his world," and found a reality, a hidden new possibility which both unmasked the ideological character of the dominant society and demanded a real revolution in order to bring it into being, since the presuppositions of the dominant society, which accounted humanity equal to "white men," did not take this black humanity into account.

This experience of "stepping outside the world" to experience a new possibility that stands in fundamental judgment upon present existence is thus the fundamental character of a counter-culture. It has been pursued in the last decades in a variety of ways. Drugs in the street communities near universities became the context of a second wave of counter-culture.

Here was a radical sense that the very consciousness of the dominant society was fundamentally ideological. The very formation of the ego in Western societies gave birth to an enslaving consciousness that trapped us in illusory problems. Liberation must begin with "blowing our minds," with dissolving our egos in order to rescind the consciousness structure of Western objectivity and alienation from the totality of reality. The method was new, but the theme was old, going back into antiscientific thinking in the romantic movement, and, beyond that, making contact with traditional mysticism. But drugs have proved themselves an illusory path, too much a part of the very manipulative, scientific culture against which they purported to protest. Most importantly, it became evident that drugs gave only an illusory experience of ego-transcendence, one which, because it was not built on real psychic maturation and development, could not in any way be built into a new self. Indeed, repeated use led to a deterioration of sensitivity rather than heightened awareness, the very opposite of the effect of real inner development.[8]

A similar denouement is pending with the theme of sexual liberation in the counter-culture. Over against a machine culture, free sexual expression seemed to be the thing that reconnected man to the earth, to his "natural self." A puritan-prurient culture of hypocrisy would be shattered by the rediscovery of the innocent sensuality of the Garden of Eden. But gradually a very old truth has begun to dawn on the movement for sexual liberation, especially as that is critically evaluated from the perspective of the liberation of women. We again discover that it is "sin," not "sex," that is our problem, and because of man's basic loss of humanity indicated by the word "sin," neither sex nor lack of sex is of any avail, but only a "new creature," to paraphrase St. Paul.

Since man is mired in inhumanity, either free use of sex, or repression of sex can equally become vehicles for expressing and promoting inhumanity. Thus both the drug element and the sexual element in the counter-culture, if pressed to their deeper conclusions, lead to a renewed grappling with the problems with which all religious spirituality has struggled, namely, the problem of inward conversion, rebirth, and spiritual development that can lead the human soul from alienation and exploitation to a life style more in communion with both cosmic reality and with the fellow human. The element of sexual sadism which is so prominent in the recent testimony by American veterans on war crimes in Vietnam makes it abundantly clear that sex cannot be a solution to war, because both sex and war are strangely intertwined in the deeper dilemma of human rapaciousness.[9]

Finally, the counter-culture today begins to settle on the more comprehensive effort to create a "new life style" and a "new community." Drugs are abandoned for an exploration of the authentic paths to a transformed consciousness. Childish "fucking" becomes restrained under a deeper sensitivity to the problems of relating sexual expression to authentic human communication and relationship. The mores of political exploitation are countered by a community which struggles with authentic democracy as self-representation in the primary forum of the local group. Economic and ecological alienation are countered by a community which tries to resist the consumer society by a rediscovery of minimal and healthy needs of human existence.

The style of such a community becomes far more ascetic and spartan, in a manner which discovers the roots of asceticism, not in masochistic repression, but in a harmony created through the simplification of life to its authentic needs and purposes. Such a community may become very a-political, but I believe that this too is an immaturity. Political maturity for such a group is approached when it realizes that its counter-culture must also become a responsible counter-culture, concerned to speak a message and spread an alternative possibility to an embattled society increasingly the victim of its own multiple idolatries.[10]

I believe that this search can properly be held to be religious if we understand religion as precisely man's search to renew his contact with the ultimate foundations of his being. It is a renewal of relationship with God which, nevertheless, can only be expressed through a renewal of authentic relationship to himself, his fellow person and created reality. Religion is a search for healing and wholeness that comes with being in communion with the transcendent source and purpose of one's being. But this transcendence is not objectifiable as a thing among things. This is why it is more authentically spoken about as the ultimate symbol of those dynamic "transcendences" which we experience in our transcendence of self-limitation in relationship to our constituted culture, identity and history. It is both a presence of a "beyond in our midst" that fills us with a proleptic experience of wholeness, but also an absence that keeps us ever searching and struggling, drawing us on to that "still more" which is "not yet." [11]

There are two ways to falsely appropriate the transcendent and so to abolish its tension and challenge. One way is to domesticate it as the established religion of the *status quo* which sanctifies things as they are. The other way is to separate out the transcendent from the whole of human life as a kind of special place which man comes to only by departing from the living and dying, loving and hating of real life. Transcendence thus cut off from real life, becomes an "otherness," in a mythologically objectified sense, which is no longer seen as intersecting, judging and transforming real life. The heavenly ceases to stand as a mandate and demand laid upon the creation. Rather God's Kingdom becomes simply the far-off heaven, rather than being, as Jesus taught us, this earth itself when God's will is done on earth. Both the establishment of Christianity and the segregation of the sacred to a sphere removed from the midst of life are equally ways of abolishing the presence of the Holy Spirit, so that the world of the powers and principalities can go on as before.

There is another alternative to these ways of relating religion to society which I believe is more authentic. This is the relationship which we find in Old Testament prophecy where the spokesman for the transcendent stands simultaneously within the social covenant and over against the ruling structures of king and temple priesthood. This doesn't make king or priesthood alien by nature to God's will, for they, too, stand within the covenant and so within the mandate of heaven. They indeed are the ones who are specifically commanded to see to the doing of God's will on earth, as it is in heaven.

But it is not automatically presumed that they do so. Their mandate does not confer an automatic blessing on their works (or pomps). Rather, beyond them, there stands the prophet whose task is to be the critical force which brings down ever anew the word of judgment and the renewed vision of what God demands that man should be. It is only by finding the way to remain within this dialectic of tension and relationship that the religious and moral counter-culture can become a healing force for man in society, without separating out into irrelevant alienation, nor yet simply selling out to bless the bombs of the dominant society.

This same analysis of the relationship of the connection between prophecy and the transcendent to society should apply to the Church as the prophetic community. The Church must again and again drop the prophetic plumb line of Hosea to find out where the crisis between obedience and disobedience is occurring so it may take its stance in relationship to the existing situation as a critical counter-culture, without copping out either through separation or through capitulation. Perhaps today something of the same kind of dialectic should also be posed in terms of the relationship of the university to society.

An authentic prophetic counter-culture then occurs wherever the protest is raised against what man has become in the name of what man is called to be, in the name of that "Kingdom come" where God's will is done on earth. Wherever this vision and protest are translated into a counter-community, ideology and life style, we have a counter-culture which is potentially redeeming. In order to be so, however, the counter-culture must hold on to two ways of relating to society simultaneously. It must lend itself and its critique to a massive and practical effort to transform the structures of the dominant society so that a greater currency of human love can be lived in and through them. This it must do in the name of human survival itself. And yet, while lending itself to the most practical and pastoral ministry to transform the structures of man to better accord with the will of heaven, it must also retain some separate identity, some way-of-being over against and in tension with, not only the currency of the old society, but any new society which it itself may help to create. Thus it can remain the critical spokesman for envisioning and experiencing that "still more" which is not yet achieved, and for glimpsing more perfect communion with the True, Good and Beautiful.

Can the new counter-culture succeed in this task where historical churches and universities have failed? Looking at their present state of immaturity, one could only doubt it. But, looking at the disaster that looms over the very existence of man on earth today, one must say that they, or something like them, had better grow up to the point where they can do it, for that *this be done* is the last thread of hope that separates us from several possible forms of hell.

On the one side, there looms the new and very possible apocalypse of military and/or ecological annihilation. On the other side, there lies the living death of the ultimate enslavement of man to his own machinery. Cosmic explosion, slow famine on a teeming, polluted earth, choking on our own excrement, or rigidification in the prison house of 1984: [12] these are the future destinies to which our present trends and technological rationality are leading us, a strange end indeed to that myth of progress which inspired those who set modern man on his way several centuries ago.

Thus the youth of today do not struggle against mere flesh and blood, but against powers and principalities, against cosmic forces so huge and so deeply entrenched that their removal by any puny efforts of mere humans seems impossible. No wonder that their efforts often seem so desperate and prone to "extremism," for the struggle is indeed one of desperation and ultimate extremes, and those who struggle are often very young, only recently awakened to the existence of evil in the world, and woefully deserted by their guilty elders. The wonder is not that a few capitulate to "extremes," but that so many keep their heads and continue to work on penultimates, having once fixed their eyes on the face of this many-horned apocalyptic beast.

If man is to prevail, and prevail in a world in which it is humanly worthwhile to prevail, it is not only advisable, but essential that this counter-culture grow into a massive body that can throw itself against this locomotive which is hurling toward the abyss to turn it around and even fundamentally restructure the character of the vehicle and of the track itself. "If man does not live by bread alone, still less does he live by disinfectants alone." We must win our way back to a world where all men can eat good bread and break bread in a way that can make it a communion with our brothers, with our mother the earth and our father the sky, and the Creator who makes all things blessed.

This simple fulness of human life is now so far removed from many of us that to find our way back to it we will have to break up and transform the form and fabric of that technological society which is presently creeping over the whole earth substituting for it an alternative whose nature we do not know and can scarcely envision except in the most fragmentary and inchoate way. Today, far more than in the era when Christ was born, a question mark lies over the whole project of human civilization. Man's house is deeply shaken. His values are thrown into question. His sins exposed. His very life totters on the brink of annihilation. Yet these death throes may yet be messianic birth pangs of a new humanity to come. "And what rough beast is this, its hour come round at last, that slouches toward Bethlehem to be born?" (Yates, "The Second Coming.")

NOTES

1. Theodore Roszak, *The Making of a Counter-Culture* (New York: Doubleday, 1970), pp. 205ff.

2. Paul Goodman, *The New Reformation* (New York: Random House, 1970).

3. See especially C. G. Jung, *The Structure and Dynamics of the Psyche* (Bollingen series, Princeton, 1969), pp. 139-236.

4. On the development of apocalyptic messianism from Jewish prophecy, see especially Sigmund Mowinckel, *He Who Cometh* (Oxford: Basil Blackwell Co., 1956). There are many studies of the character of Jewish apocalyptic, but only recently, through the study of writing such as the "War Between the Sons of Light and the Sons of Darkness" of the Dead Sea Scrolls and the study of zealotism, have Christians found it necessary to begin to recognize apocalypticism as the literature of the Jewish resistance movement to Roman imperialism that began with the Maccabees and culminated in the Jewish Wars. See, for example, Yigael Yadin, *The Scrolls of the War Between the Sons of Light and the Sons of Darkness* (Oxford, U. P., 1962). Also G. R. Driver, *The Judean Scrolls* (Oxford, Basil Blackwell, 1965).

5. The best study of gnosticism as a religious expression of alienation is that of Hans Jonas, *The Gnostic Religion: The Message of the Alien God* (Boston: Beacon, 1958).

6. See, for example, S. L. Greenslade, *Church and State From Constantine to Theodosius* (London: SCM. Press, 1954) for a study of this development. The Anabaptists of the sixteenth century Reformation were the first to raise the idea of a fundamental "fall" of Christianity through the Constantinian establishment, but this idea has been increasingly adopted in the nineteenth and twentieth centuries among churches that once belonged to established tradition, as the separation of church and state and secularism created a new consciousness of the new challenge of a "post-Constantinian" church.

7. Martin Buber, *I and Thou* (Edinburgh: T. and T. Clark, 1937).

8. This kind of critique is increasingly frequent in the underground press. See, for example, Allen Cohen, "Acid and the Search for God," from the *Catonsville Roadrunner*, reprinted in *Win Magazine*, February 1971, pp. 6-8.

9. See Leah Fritz's article "Out of the Test Tube, Endlessly Fucking," in *Win Magazine*, February 1971, pp. 9-11.

10. The New Left has tended primarily in the direction of the anarcho-utopian tradition of socialism, rather than toward Marxism. Increasingly writers of the New Left are exploring their own historical roots in the thought of nineteenth century anarchists, such as Proudhon and Kropotkin. One of the older mentors of New Left communitarianism is Paul Goodman. See his *Communitas: Means of Livelihood and Ways of Life* (New York: Random House, 1969).

11. In his *Theology of Hope* (New York: Harpers, 1967), Jürgen Moltmann attacks the theology of transcendent immanence, which he identifies with Rudolf Bultmann's existentialism, in contrast to his own stress on the absent and "coming" God. However, this stress on the "not yet," at the expense of all sense of immanent communion with the "beyond in our midst" seems equally one-sided. The myth of the "above" and the myth of the "beyond" are complementary aspects of man's experience of transcendence, the one in relationship to being and the other in relationship to becoming and history. It would seem that a catholic theology would have to find a way of affirming both experiences.

12. The literature on the coming "catastrophe" in such areas as population explosion, militarism and the arms race, ecology, technology and urban society is extensive. One would recommend such titles as Herbert York, *Race to Oblivion* (New York: Simon

and Shuster, 1970); Lewis Mumford, *The Myth of the Machine and the Pentagon of Power* (New York: Harcourt and Brace, 1970); Robert Lifton, *Thought Reform and the Psychology of Totalism* (New York: Norton, 1961); Semour Melman, *Our Depleted Society* (New York: Delta, 1966); *Eco-Catastrophe*, by the editors of Ramparts (New York: Harpers, 1970); and Herbert Marcuse, *One-Dimensional Man* (Boston: Beacon, 1964).

Chapter 3

The Vanishing Religious Order and the Emerging Human Community

It should come as no surprise, to those who have been watching developments in the Catholic Church recently, that we seem to have entered a time of the vanishing religious order. This poses a peculiar problem for those whose job it is to recruit new members for traditional religious structures. Even creative criticism may come to be received with much less enthusiasm, when it is no longer clearly pointing to revival and new "success" for these structures even if updated, but rather appears to be only hastening their liquidation. Many Catholics doubtless are a little dazed to discover that the Church, in its various institutional forms, once taken as so immovable, now appears to be so easy to destroy. Who would have thought, even ten years ago, that those mountains of tradition would take such a few pushes to send them sliding down toward the sea? Perhaps this simply means that the immobility concealed what was really a lack of resiliency. The facade looked impregnable, but this really meant that the power for rebirth was weak. Yet the fact is that it has been precisely those orders which have been boldest and most creative in adaptation which now seem threatened with extinction. Like Cheshire cats, they seem to be fading into insubstantiality, beginning with the tips of their tails and ending with the grin, which remains for some time after the rest of the cat has gone. The whole problem of renewing religious orders is clearly proving more problematical than even the boldest of reformers would have thought only a few years ago. The gap between the presuppositions on which orders were built and maintained and what is taken to be relevant Christianity today is very wide. If we really want to get there, many in religious orders are beginning to think that "we probably just shouldn't start from here."

But my message is not primarily one of doom. It is instead one of surprising new possibilities, if we are creative enough to grasp them. As the form of religious orders begins to fade, we may get a brief look at what their original content was all about. There may be a much greater demand for this content today than there has been for many generations, but it will be a demand only for those who are free enough to stop hanging on to the remnants of traditional forms and ready to start over again where the message itself is being sought, and let new forms grow up organically around this new search. In other words, I see tremendous possibilities for both covenanted communities of personal commitment and social concern, and also possibilities for new forms of contemplative life, but only for those who are not afraid to dissolve much of what they once thought were their "religious" identities.

Let us try to understand this problem by looking for a moment at the historical development of religious orders. Monasticism arose in the Church at the time of the Constantinian establishment, and it operated as a reaction to this domestication of the Church within the social order of "the world." In the first centuries of the Church's life, to enter the Christian community was itself to leave the mainstream of society and enter a new community of personal rebirth, risk and commitment. But when the ordinary Christian congregation became simply a unit of normative society, when being a Christian was even required as part of being a good citizen, joining a Christian congregation ceased to express a personal decision and commitment transcendent to the life style of the social *status quo*. It was then that monastic communities sprang up to fill the role which had once been played by the local Christian congregation. To seek Christian perfection now was seen as a higher calling and an elite group beyond the ordinary baptized Christian. One now thought of being a "religious" as something higher than being a "Christian," whereas previously the two were simply one and the same. Some connection between the two was preserved in the fourth century by having the "ordinary Christian" remain a catechumen until his deathbed, whereas the one who made the special commitment to seek perfection would then be baptized and enter monastic life. The highest Christian ethic was still seen as founded upon baptism. But, as infant baptism became widespread, the decision to live the converted life came to be seen as a new elite with a higher calling than the baptized.

This quest for Christian perfection originally had little to do with either intellectual cultivation or social mission. It was understood in ascetic, contemplative terms, as withdrawal from the "flesh" and the "world" into a detached "spiritual" state. Its ethic was much closer to Plato who speaks of the philosopher living the life of "mortification"; that is, the practice of dying, or the withdrawal of the soul from the body, than it was to the Sermon on the Mount. It was in the context of this ascetic ethic that celibacy was assumed to be intrinsic to Christian perfection, Monastic life in the Eastern Church has remained close to this ascetic, contemplative vision, but in the West it has increasingly departed from it. With the collapse of educational institutions in the fifth century the monk was recruited as copyist, librarian and teacher, and the monastic order became the key institution for the transmission of learning; something which had been no part of its original conception. With the advent of the preaching orders of the thirteenth century, the order broke with its contemplative form and entered the "active life" of social mission. All this meant that celibacy had less and less to do with its original context within

an ascetic, contemplative ethic, and instead was continued,
and even extended to the secular clergy, primarily as an institutional virtue. Impersonal institutions, whether armies,
prisons, or orders can regiment and deploy people better if
they are separated from family relationships and can be dealt
with as isolated units. To be sure, the ideals of the eschatological ethic continued to be used to justify celibacy, but in actual
life style, celibacy increasingly lost any connection with a life
of special risk, insecurity and tension with the social *status quo*.
Indeed, it came to function institutionally as the exact negation
of such an eschatological ethic; as a way of stabilizing people
as much as possible by cutting them off from intellectual, emotional or social risk, or insecurity.

Today it seems to me that there is a significant rebirth of
an eschatological ethic among Christians. But those who decide
to enter communities of special risk, commitment and tension
with the worldly social order, far from becoming celibate on
doing so, seem rather to do the opposite; they leave religious
orders and get married. To depart from the social *status quo*
to a new life of commitment and service is also seen as entering a community of close personal commitments, which may
include marriage with another person who also shared this
special commitment, although this marriage itself is seen as a
part of the larger community of risk and service. It is true that
some theoreticians among Christian radicals, such as the Berrigan brothers, feel that celibacy now acquires a new meaning as
a life style of freedom for risk, but, in practice, there has been
no such definitive relationship between the two. It is partly due
to the fact that marriage today has much less to do with en-
tangling economic and social obligations than it did in the past,
and so interferes much less with people's freedom for drastic
risk and change, while it offers the sustaining human relationship
which many people are finding to be the essential psychic
foundation for maintaining a life style of tension and risk
vis á vis the larger society. In his *Letters and Papers from
Prison*, Dietrich Bonhoeffer remarks that he once thought that
celibacy would be an aid to one who was imprisoned, but in
actuality he found that the most important thing to him when

in prison was his family and especially his relationship with his fiancée. I suspect that the Berrigan family may have found a similar closeness in the same situation.

What I am suggesting is that today we are rediscovering something of the meaning of an eschatological ethic and an eschatological community. This is the prophetic community which lives on the transcendent edge between the dominant society and some "new world" which is about to be born. It is the community of both judgment and redeeming grace which lives in a tension with the present dehumanized form of life and in expectation of a new world to come. This was the witness originally carried by the monastic community, although in practice it cultivated a life style that less and less witnessed in any credible way to this content. But this concept of the eschatological community is not the special preserve of the "religious" community; rather is it precisely the real meaning of the Church itself! If religious orders are disappearing, it may be because this inner content is being rediscovered as the normative content of the local Christian congregation, much the way it was rediscovered as the normal meaning of the Church by the religious radicals of the sixteenth century (i.e. the Anabaptists). Constantinianism, which once separated the "religious" community from the local congregation, itself is disappearing. Less and less are people baptized automatically as a way of registering their birth, nor do they go to church simply as a social obligation. True, there are many churches which still operate in this way, but they are in a static state. The dynamism of a new Christianity is carried by those for whom baptism or personal commitment in faith means living in tension and prophetic witness toward the dominant society and entering a new kind of community which cultivates this witness and commitment as its life style. But this new community is no longer seen as an "order" or a "religious" community, separate or higher than the Christian community. It is simply the Church or the Christian community itself in its normative form. And so the disappearance of religious orders as separate structures may be simply the other side of a convergence of religious orders with new Christian communities, which see a life of high commitment and service as the normative life style of a Christian congregation. Moreover, neither the institutionalized territorial parish nor the institutionalized religious order really expressed such values of community or of service. Their life style was deliberately impersonal, and their work focused primarily on institutional self-preservation rather than free or prophetic service. And so the search of people in both of these institutions for renewal has brought them to a point of convergence where they are about to bump into each other in the fog and recognize that they are both engaged in a search for the same concept of Christian community. This new form of expressing real Christian community will necessarily break with the institutional forms which have grown up around both the territorial parish and the religious order, and this becomes necessary precisely as both seek the real meaning and content of their own original purpose. This doesn't mean that everyone from both sides of this convergence will necessarily arrive at exactly the same solution. One might have here a community of celibates, and there a community of married people and children, and someplace else a mixed community of married people, children and single people. One might have some communities that are more open to a rapid change of membership, and others which demand a more long-term covenant between a specific group of people. Some communities may concentrate more on social mission, and others more on personal relationships and the cultivation of the interior life. But in every case, they will cease to regard themselves as some higher "state of life" separate from the congregation of the baptized Christian, and rather come to see themselves simply as forms of the local church, just as the Christian congregation itself should cease to see itself as a passive recipient of sacramental ministrations from those on a higher plane than themselves, and their members will cease to join churches simply as a way of participating in the civic *status quo*. Instead people will see the joining of a Christian congregation as a way of entering a new life style in common with a community that shares this commitment to a new humanity.

Side by side with this convergence of the religious order

and the local congregation on the root meaning of Christian community, we also find a second kind of convergence which is radically altering the style of personal relationships of those in institutions known as "celibate religious orders" and those who belong to that state of life known as "marriage." For large numbers of those who made some commitment to the priesthood or the religious order some years ago, the ethic of celibacy is eroding, or rather, we should say it is proving to have less and less to do with the real content of that commitment. We have seen that celibacy arose originally within a monastic concept of religious life, where it was integral to an ascetic, contemplative definition of Christian perfection. But this has long since ceased to be the actual life style of most Western religious orders. Moreover, the essential anthropology presumed by celibacy, or rather by the ethic of "virginity" (which isn't necessarily the same thing as celibacy), is being rejected, and rejected especially by those who are most active in the renewal of the Christian community ethic. We are now inclined to believe that we relate to God by relating to our brothers and sisters, not by detaching ourselves from other people. We are inclined to think that life without love, without deep friendship and personal relationships, is less than an authentic human life, that sexual relationship is a normal dimension of human relationship and that Christian perfection cannot mean anything if it is contrary to humanization. Thus throughout the religious orders today we find people searching for what is called "the third way," whereby the dimension of friendship between men and women as a normal and essential part of human development can be cultivated without breaking with the outward form of celibate life.

I personally find a lot of the conversation on this subject that I hear from people in religious life highly problematical. There is something here suggestive of a kind of charade, as though it were simply a matter of retaining the external formalities of celibate life, at least somewhere short of taking out the marriage license and packing one's bags in the local religious residence, while largely evacuating the meaning of that concept of man and that concept of life which was the *raison d'être* for this life style. I am afraid that the new way, may, for many people, turn out to be hardly distinguishable from some very "old ways" indeed! To pursue sexual relationship as a form of "humanization" without personal responsibility may become little more than a sophisticated rationalization for some very traditional kinds of exploitation. If people are honest, I suspect they will realize, that in order to develop new kinds of human relationships, they may have to break, not only with previous interpretations, but also with some conventional forms of celibate life. They will have to seek new forms of socialization that are more honestly appropriate to this new content.

But is marriage really the only alternative to celibacy, at least as marriage has been traditionally defined; in terms of child-raising, private property, private wage earning, an exclusive, lifelong relationship between two people, etc? In short, is the sort of economic, social and personal relationships associated with marriage the only moral option for sexual, love relationships between men and women? What we are finding today is that, as celibate life breaks out of its ascetic mold and rationale, so also family life is going through a complementary morphological shift. The younger generation is becoming convinced that the nuclear family cannot be sustained. The advent of women's liberation has disinclined many women to accepting the sequestered life in the home where they are no longer free to relate to any man except their husband, and through him, their husband's friends. Economically and socially, the nuclear family is proving to be too narrow a unit, confining the wife to a strange existence as a household serf, solely responsible for the maintenance of the household and isolated from contact with other adults. We should not confuse this kind of nuclear family with some eternal essence of marriage and family life. It is a comparatively modern development which has destroyed older extended forms of family life in which grandmothers, aunts and other adults lived with the family and the father's work was much more closely related to the household. Many young people today are revolting against this kind of isolated unit as necessary either for marriage or child raising. People are seeking relationships which can express love, commitment and responsibility, but in a more open and less exclusive form. People are more mobile today, and they expect to relate to larger groups on less than a lifetime basis. People are seeking forms of community which can include something more like a tribe, but made up of a peer group, which can express such values as shared social concern and social action, shared reading, shared prayer, shared economic life, shared fun and relaxation, and shared housekeeping and child-raising. The commune is the small but growing option to the nuclear family for such people today.

It is fairly easy to see how a commune can get together a group of friends, living together, sharing housekeeping and expenses. It is more difficult to see how it can integrate the sexual dimension of this relationship. Groups that have tried plural sexual relations have not had a happy experience with it although there have been some, such as the nineteenth century utopian community of Oneida in New York State, which developed a successful ethos of plural sexual relationships. Most communes, however, seem to end up with a functional monogamy among its members, although not necessarily in terms of life-long commitment. Whether this is due simply to our social conventions or is really intrinsic to the "nature" of sexuality seems to me to be an open question. I don't think we can make snap judgments without a much more careful understanding of the relationship of human sexuality to loving. Moreover, it seems to me to be a subject upon which most of the traditions of Catholic moral theology, whether the old anti-sexual variety, or the new kind which extols sexuality as a kind of total sacramental communion, are not very helpful. Most of those cliches need to be cleared out of the way in order to look at human relationships in a more humane and a more realistic way. The communes are groping in considerable uncertainty as to the implications for sexual relations of peer-group communities. But they are searching in the name of good moral values, and consequently such experimentation cannot be dismissed simply as "sin." At the same time this development can be seen as converging with a complementary search among those in religious life for a fuller humanization which does not exclude the sexual nature of people.

We have been speaking of this convergence of the religious order and the local church, and also the religious community and the familial community, primarily in terms of a social ethic. Most of those engaged in this convergence in search of a new human community are committed to a social ethic of challenge and change *vis à vis* the forms of contemporary bourgeois technological society. Their ethic is directed outward toward social criticism of dehumanizing forms of social, political and economic relations. But today we also find a new search for contemplation and the deeper interior life among many of those engaged in this search for the new human community. Ironically, the religious groups have probably been less involved in this new search for interior life than the secular side of the movement. Mysticism is bigger with hippies than it is with monks it seems! There is a newly awakened sense of a need for contemplation, interior integration and a new consciousness of the transcendent foundations of individual existence that has been awakened precisely among those who have been most completely secularized. By and large the monastic orders, originally created to serve this need, have not had the form or the style to respond to this new demand. As Thomas Merton remarked, "when the Beatles went in search of contemplation, they sought out an Indian guru, and not the monks of Gethsemane." People do want some kind of contemplation and transcendent experience, but not as a lifelong career or something which requires that they detach themselves from human relationships and social concerns. They want it as a dimension of the totality of life, and not as an exclusive preoccupation. In India, for example, withdrawal to a monastery is seen as one of the stages of life, alongside of others, such as the student stage of life, and the married, householder stage of life. Contemplation is a vocation open to everyone as one dimension of life, rather than an exclusive vocation for a few. Western monasticism needs to develop something of this broader definition of the contemplative calling. In a similar way communities seeking the integration of the values of social mission, loving friendship between men and women and moral growth also want to integrate the dimension of prayer and contemplation into an understanding of the full human community. This is no longer "religious" life, as opposed to "secular" life. It is no longer "married" as radically different from "single" life. It is no longer "clerical" as opposed to the "lay" state of life. But it is simply what fully human life in community is all about. It seems to me this is the sort of search that people are making today. And every traditional institution, whether it be the religious order, the local church or the family, is engaged in a process of challenge, convergence and mutual transformation in this common search for ways of understanding and expressing what "life together" is all about.

Chapter 4
Is Celibacy Eschatological?
The Suppression of
Christian Radicalism

The ethic which has supported a celibate ministry in Western Christianity for sixteen centuries is breaking down. The chorus of voices demanding a change in this discipline is rising. Yet most of the sociological studies on this subject skirt the theological foundations of this discipline in Christian history. For this reason odd rags and tags of the old presuppositions survive to prevent a coherent critique from emerging. One hears, for example, from those priests who have broken psychologically with the relationship between ordination and celibacy, the statement that "they don't happen to have this particular gift." It is implied that this gift is indeed a "wonderful thing to have," for those privileged to receive it, but, for some reason, they are not among those so privileged, and, in any case, it is not at all normative for the Christian ministry. By a peculiar sleight of hand, the whole ethic of celibacy is thus made mysterious to any knowable values and hence irrelevant. Yet one saves face for those still committed to it by talking obscurely about a "gift" given to a "few," "for the sake of the Kingdom" that is indeed precious, although irrelevant to most people, and so can thereafter be dismissed from any bearing on one's own ideals.

What kind of a "gift" is this? Why would the "Holy Spirit" want to do something like that to someone? What is the Holy Spirit doing anyway? Mysteriously dropping a blight of impotence on a few "pour encourager les autres," to quote the famous line from Voltaire's *Candide?* Does the Holy Spirit perhaps go about secretively lowering the natural libido of a certain elected group of people, so they have lower levels of sexual energy than others and so can "remain continent"? Or perhaps does he lay such a heavy grip of sexual fear upon these few (obviously with a little help from certain ecclesiastical institutions) that they can successfully wall themselves away from experiencing that need? With a divine Friend like that, who needs an enemy? Can there be a special, arcane ethic reserved for a few that doesn't relate at all to the economy of humanization normative for Christians as a whole? What is this special grace that is the enemy of natural life? What is this "Way to Heaven" which is the enemy of the processes of creation? Does the God of the "other world" cancel out the God who made the world in the beginning and saw that it was "very good?" These are some of the theological questions raised by the idea of celibacy as a special and higher gift of the Holy Spirit reserved for the few in a way that is not normatively related to either the Christian ministry or to Christian life. Such language about celibacy is thrown into jeopardy when it is no longer regarded as an ideal for the converted Christian generally and becomes confined to an obscure corner to be honored by a quick nod of the head and then passed by to go about those things which are really seen as normatively conducive to good human (Christian) life.

The defense of celibacy by those who remain committed to it has become similarly frayed and tattered. It is common for the liberal cleric to concede that celibacy indeed is not normative for all priests, but to add something vague about celibacy as more conducive to "full-time ministry." Such "full-time commitment" is then blessed with language about being "totally devoted to the building of the Kingdom," which those who are not similarly undivided cannot achieve to the same degree. But what does a monolithic devotion to a particular set of professional services in the ecclesiastical institution have to do with being either "eschatological" or "building the Kingdom"? (This is not unlike the question that used to occur to me as a child when the Sunday preacher would urge us to give a part of our money "to God." I used to think to myself, "What makes you think giving my money to *you* is equivalent to giving it to God?"). More specifically, why wouldn't a more pluralistic life style, which includes many relationships; which incorporates love, friendship, marriage, child-raising, professional, social, political and cultural concerns, be a better image of that full-bodied life that might "build the Kingdom" than a monolithic devotion to such a profession? Is there something about being "one-sided" that is particularly heavenly? Would perhaps being a full-time militarist, doctor, convict, mental patient or racketeer be similarly "eschatological?" Any one of these pursuits might similarly suggest or even force one to opt for the unmarried life in order to inhabit a totalistic institution or pursue a demanding career that calls for the exclusive devotion of time and energy.

The notion that one is better equipped to pursue a ministry "full time" because one is unmarried is itself a questionable proposition. Everyone has much the same needs for sleep, food, recreation and companionship, whether one is single or married. The typical high level executive who works at his job with single-minded devotion is probably much more "full time" in his work than the typical celibate priest. An analysis of what a parish priest actually does with his time each day, in contrast with either married ministers or professionals with demanding vocations, would quickly reveal the meaninglessness of this proposition of "full time" ministry among the celibate. But it is much more important to ask why such a notion has been seen as having anything to do with living a redemptive life style and why it is so peculiarly labeled "eschatological."

A year or so ago this author attended a meeting of the Bishop's liaison committee and the leaders of the Society of Priests for a Free Ministry (who advocate a married priesthood and de-clericalized life styles for the ministry). Bishop Bernardin was perhaps the most open of the committee members in trying to discuss the issues. At one point the bishop defended the normative character of celibacy by stating that it was required by the New Testament. I replied that this was not the case, quoting passages from the Pastoral Epistles which show that the New Testament concept of the Church was modeled after the Jewish family, the normative requirements for the ministry being identical with those which make for a good father, husband and family man. Marriage, not celibacy, is regarded as normative for the presbyter and bishop. Sensing perhaps that his acquaintance with Scripture was too shaky to enter into debate on this ground, the bishop withdrew to the higher ground of spirituality and spoke eloquently of celibacy as "eschatological." I replied that, actually, celibacy was in considerable tension with the ethic of Kingdom-building, in its present Roman institutionalized form. In this form, it was much closer to the ethic of totalitarian institutions, such as prisons, armies and mental institutions, which similarly demand a monolithic and total control over their members that excludes inter-personal relationships. The bishop then simply declared that the bishops were totally committed to celibacy, that we might as well know that they would not hear of any criticism of it, and that was that.

Clearly, here we have a practice that has lost its original rationale so completely that even its firmest defenders can no longer remember what it is all about. The defenses of it preserve scraps and pieces of a once mighty and coherent, albeit (in my view) incorrect, idea of man and the cosmos, which has collapsed. These bits and pieces, when cited outside the context of this original world view, no longer have any real meaning or point of reference. Let us return to the roots of this world view and reconstruct briefly that anthropology and cosmology in which celibacy might appear as the normative ethic of "salvation," not only for priests and "religious," but for all truly converted Christians.

The word "eschatological" comes from the Greek word

"eschaton" which means "the end"; i.e., the end of the world, or the apocalyptic overthrow of the spatial-temporal creation and its replacement with a heavenly world beyond space and time. This idea had faded to the periphery of Christian theology in modern times, until it was revived by Biblical scholarship. It was redeemed from its embarrassing mythological literalism by scholars such as Rudolf Bultmann, who demythologized it and interpreted the "eschatological" as an interworldly ethic of encounter with the Ultimate. However, it is doubtful whether this modernizing interpretation fully preserves the dilemma toward finite creation and its redeemability posed by literal eschatological thinking. Moreover, the New Testament scholars must seriously rethink the current assumption that the word "eschatological" is equivalent to "Christological" or "messianic." A study of the actual development of the messianic idea in Judaism will reveal the tenuousness of identifying the "messianic" concept with a late apocalyptic idea of an "eschatology beyond history."

Hebrew messianic hope was futuristic, but this-worldly. Its hope was for the fulfillment of creation, not for its abolition. The vision of the future messianic age in the prophets assumes that there will be marrying, birth and death and all the other life processes in the Kingdom. Only the disorder of sin and apostasy from God's will shall be overcome:

> For behold I create a new Heaven and a new Earth, and the former things shall not be remembered or come to mind. But be glad and rejoice forever in that which I create. For behold I create Jerusalem a rejoicing and her people a joy . . . No more shall be heard in it the sound of weeping and the cry of distress. No more shall there be in it an infant that lives but a few days, or an old man who does not fill out his days . . . They shall build houses and inhabit them, They shall plant vineyards and eat of their fruit. . . . for like the days of a tree shall the days of my people be, and my chosen shall long enjoy the work of their hands. They shall not labor in vain, or bear children in calamity, for they shall be the offspring of the blessed of the Lord, and their children with them.
>
> Isaiah 65: 17-23.

The messianic age is not one of flight from earth to heaven, but rather that time and place where God's will is done on earth, as it is in heaven. Heaven is not a supernatural "place" to which one goes by abolishing the earth, but it is the mandate for what ought to be done on earth.

However, during the period from the Maccabees to the Jewish Wars (200 B.C. to 100 A.D.), a change took place in the messianic tradition in Judaism. Under the pressure of repeated experiences of imperial conquest and the frustration of all hopes of liberation as an autonomous nation, Israel's messianic hope became more and more radicalized and cut off from continuity with finite created and social life. Not only sin, but the very limits of finite spatiotemporal reality came to be seen as an obstacle to the fulfillment of human hope. This view is expressed in the apocalyptic writings of the inter-testamental period. It is Christianity that carried on this apocalyptic tradition and the literature in which it was developed. Rabbinic Judaism after the fall of Jerusalem repudiated this apocalyptic literature.

The apocalypses were influenced by two strains of dualistic thinking; Persian dualism, with its view of world history as a struggle between a good and an evil cosmic power, ending in the overthrow of finite creation and the establishment of a new super-mundane world beyond history; and Greek dualism with its division of reality into matter and spirit; the mutable and the immutable. Only with the incorporation of these two alien forms of dualism into messianic, futuristic thinking, did Jewish future hope come to define the "age to Come" as one which is super-mundane and eternal and arises after the end of this world. Yet even this development did not abolish this worldly messianic hope. Rather it created a bifurcation in this hope, where a this-worldly millennium was expected, to be followed by an eternal world after the end of history. Christ, in the Jewish apocalypses, was defined as the militant warrior king of the millennial age, whereas no messiah at all is needed in the eternal age, but only the direct reign of God. The same idea underlies the dual kingdoms of Revelations 19:11-22,5. In Judaism, messianic thinking ultimately differentiated itself from eschatological thinking and cannot be seen as necessarily identical with it.

It is improper to say that such an apocalyptic hope produced a celibate ethic within Judaism. The apocalyptic sects in the time of Jesus did not seem to have practiced celibacy. The view that the Essenes were celibate comes from Josephus (*The Jewish War II,* 8: 2,13). But Josephus is known to assimilate the description of the Jewish sects into the characteristics of Greek philosophical sects for the sake of making them palatable to the Hellenistic world. If the sect described by Philo in his treatise "on the Contemplative Life" is an offshoot of the Essenes, it is clear that it has entirely lost the apocalyptic orientation of the *Dead Sea Scrolls* and has translated the Jewish idea of the future age into Greek philosophical dualism. It is in this context that celibacy becomes an "eschatological ethic." But the Essene community in Palestine, which lived in militant expectation of the dawning of the Kingdom of God, shows in its own writings to have expected its members to be married (*Zadokite Document,* vii,6). The Zealots show no evidence of having practiced celibacy. Whether these militant apocalypticists are to be regarded as one group or not is a matter of some dispute, but, in any case, the final stand of the *Sicarii* at Masada at the end of the Jewish wars found these messianic guerrilla warriors living in a fortress community not unlike that found at Qumran, together with their wives and children, all of whom committed suicide together rather than submit to the Romans (Josephus, *The Jewish War,* VII,8).

A messianic ethic in such a context of apocalyptic expectation was one of risk and insecurity, not one of anti-sexuality. Such an ethic did not suppose that a man would not marry and have children, but rather that, having these as normative Jewish family life, he would nevertheless be forced in the time of final crisis to "leave his wife and child" and "take to the hills." That is, in the time of ultimate world crisis before the coming of the messianic Kingdom, the "saints" would have to sever the ties and security that linked them to the ordinary life of society and take to the life of repentance and guerrilla resistance in the caves and desert areas of Judea, such as were cultivated by the Essenes, the *Sicarii* and the various desert prophets, such as John the Baptist. This is probably the kind of messianic ethic of risk and insecurity that is intended by the apocalyptic passages of the synoptic gospels (Matthew 24: 2-26; Mark 13: 5-27; Luke 21: 8-26).

Such descriptions of leaving wife and child and all social ties for the Kingdom of God do not, however, imply the institutionalization of a childless, unmarried state. Rather, they imply the disruption of all institutional ties, by those who are presumed, normatively, to be *already married and parents*. An institutionalized celibate state, far from being the natural development of such a messianic ethic, is actually the abolition of the whole context in which such a messianic ethic was meaningful. It represents the substitution of an alternative and much more total security system for that of the family, a new security system that wards off one's ability to suffer any such risk and insecurity. The kind of messianic ethic spoken of in the apocalyptic sections of the gospels cannot be institutionalized at all, least of all by monastic life. It must be lived in the context of a real and unique crisis in particular moments in history when one is forced to disrupt all institutional ties and step outside all security systems, while still being very much torn and divided by the continuing reality of such ties in one's life. Otherwise the sundering of ties is not insecurity and risk, but rather the opposite, the abolition of the possibility of insecurity and risk.

How did the eschatological ethic come to be interpreted in terms of institutionalized celibacy? Essentially this came about through the translation of the apocalyptic dualism of historical crisis into the Greek philosophical dualism of body and soul. Heaven was no longer seen as breaking in and disrupting the order of a disobedient society, overthrowing its evil structures and creating the new possibility of a redeemed life on earth. Rather, heaven now was seen as located statically "above," as the spiritual realm that corresponds to the "soul," just as the earthly realm corresponds to body. The ethic of the Kingdom of Heaven now comes to be seen as the Platonic ethic of "mortification" (*Phaedrus* 66,67). Salvation is seen as the adoption of a death ethic of lifelong struggle to withdraw from social and physical processes and to live the "angelic life," "as though not in the body." The seeker after perfection withdrew not only from economic, political and cultural processes, but even from the physical processes of life, such as eating, sleeping, bathing, all physical enjoyment, and especially from sex, as the expression of those life processes that "keep the world going."

But such an ethic of asceticism, however, did not demand a withdrawal from the institution of marriage necessarily, strangely enough. It was sex and procreation that were to be eschewed. Both St. Jerome and St. Augustine express the opinion that, if all humanity were to follow the Christian way and cease to have children, the world would come to an end the faster and the Kingdom of Heaven would dawn. Both feel that there is no need for the Christian to have any children, since there are already enough people to populate heaven from past generations. Christians should leave carnal generation to the pagans and concentrate on the second birth of spiritual regeneration of the soul. Sex was the central symbol of that filthy carnality which draws the soul down from spiritual to fleshly things. To eschew marriage was simply the most likely way to keep away from sex. But the ascetic writers also urged the married to withdraw from sex as well and to live continent marriages. This ideal was held up, not only to the "monks" and "virgins," but to all Christians. Those who could not achieve it were regarded as third class citizens of the Church, spiritually. They lacked the full "gift" of Christian conversion to the life of the resurrection.

This cultivation of the ascetic life arose originally in the monastic movement, not as an ethic of the ordinary ministry of the Church. The presbyters and bishops of the Church continued to be married, as they had been in the first century of the Church. But, more and more, in the ascetic writers, who were the intellectual and spiritual leaders of the Church in the fourth century, there was an insistence that the ministry particularly should set the example by following this "way of perfection." Since most of the priests and bishops were married, they should, at least, practice continent marriage. This again indicates that it was not the single or unmarried state *per se,* but anti-sexuality that was the heart of the celibate ethic. Christian conversion was identified with withdrawal from all things "of the flesh" and the exclusive concentration upon that spiritual world of the soul that enabled one to live as much as possible "as though not in the body." Such a life was identified with the life of prayer. Jerome and other writers insist that the priest, whose ministry is that of constant prayer, must therefore be wholly continent. For it is impossible to pray and live sexually at the same time.

It is in the context of this world view that all the language about "being undivided," "having a full-time ministry," being exclusively devoted to "heavenly things"; celibacy as the "gift of the Holy Spirit," and as a "heavenly" or "eschatological" ethic has meaning. Once this world view and all its psychological, anthropological and theological underpinnings have evaporated, as they have for most people in contemporary Christianity, these phrases live on as odd leftovers from a world view whose *raison d'être* has disappeared. Once outside this context, such phrases have lost their original point of reference and have become contentless.

What then do we do with the institutions which we have inherited from the celibate ethic today? Can we take the form of institutionalized celibacy which we have inherited in the priesthood and the religious orders and pour a new wine of sexual liberation into them, keeping only the outward form of celibate community life, but no longer demanding that this be a sexless life? This is undoubtedly the path that many radical innovators in contemporary Catholicism would like to follow, in more or less well thought-out ways. I would suggest that such an effort to pour this kind of new wine into those kinds of old wineskins will most likely be a total institutional and personal disaster. There is simply no intellectually honest way of substituting for a celibate life, designed to safeguard the virgin life, of original asceticism, an unmarried but sexually active life and pretending in any sense that this is an authentic "development" of Christian celibacy! The Church Fathers would have had quite another name for that. They would have called it "fornication"; the lowest and most bestial form of life, cut off from all possibility of redemption, in their view. Such a practice would have fallen not only far below the shining life of virginity and the second-class life of widowed or married continence, but even far below that grudgingly conceded third-class life of procreative marriage, for the Church Fathers.

Therefore we must be clear about the radical break that is involved in the anthropology that supports a liberated sexual ethic, and the impossibility of adapting ascetic institutions and cultures to this new viewpoint in any intrinsic sense. Intellectually, there is no way to fudge oneself into a continuity between these two opposites. Neither the form nor the content of the ascetic tradition can intrinsically support such a new content. For this reason those, whom I have known, who have moved beyond sexual fantasizing and have actually attempted to adopt a sexually active life, while remaining in unchanged celibate institutional forms, have suffered destructive psychic upheavals far deeper than they expected and found no resources for guidance or healing within the culture and social form which they occupied. On the contrary, their very continuance in such a celibate institutional form itself generated guilt complexes which their new intellectual position could not readily master on the deeper psychological level.

Celibate culture derives from a view of women and sexuality which might be described as both narcissistic and sexist. Sex is viewed as "polluting" and carnal. One either shuns women or, if one "uses" them for "relief of concupiscence," this falls into a depersonalized attitude toward them that eschews real inter-personality. I have even heard it argued that a priest, who has sexual relations, still remains "celibate," as long as he is uncommitted and does not relate himself to any "one woman!" On the other hand, "valid sex," within marriage, is assimilated into a property relationship, where the body of the wife is viewed as the exclusive property of the husband, and the children seen as "proofs of virility." Those who have been deeply molded by this double tradition of narcissism and male sexism are very unlikely to be able to

break with the taboos of both marriage and celibacy simultaneously and to move directly to a sexual ethic of mature
inter-personality outside the form of marriage. The overwhelming tendency will be for such a relationship to be handled
psychologically by being lowered to that uncommitted ethic
of depersonalization of the sexual partner who is "used" for
the "relief of concupiscence" that was the traditional rationalization of clerical concubinage.

In other words, what we are saying is that the form and
culture of celibacy confine a person to attitudes and styles of
life which are incompatible with a liberated sexual personalism. One must break much more radically with the outward
forms of celibate life in order to create a new form and culture
that might be more intrinsically appropriate to a personalist
and non-sexist view of sexual relationship as a loving and
responsible relationship. What that form will be and how it
may also reshape the institution of marriage is still uncertain.
But one thing must be clear; communes cannot be readily built
from the cultural and institutional building blocks of the
celibate rectory or convent without frank and open reshaping
of their outward form and inner content. Any halfway
measures, which appear in the old form, while sneaking in a
new content, do not promote good, wholesome psyches. There
must be an open and thoroughgoing rethinking of that new
world view with all its dimensions that is truly adequate to
sustain such an alternative life style, and the shaping of a new
communal, social form that is honestly expressive of it.

What then remains of what was traditionally called "the
eschatological ethic"? Surely no one would want to rule out
the legitimate possibility of that clerical life style of monolithic
devotion to a profession, to a life of service or to a life of
prayer and study. But it is questionable whether such "single-
ness of mind" can be regarded as an ethic that is uniquely
suited to the "building of the Kingdom," in the Biblical sense
of messianic hope. The anthropology of body-soul dualism that
was the foundation of traditional asceticism contradicts a
Biblical sense of man and creation. The messianic hope for
redemption was one that redeems life in the body, rather than

merely fleeing from bodily life. The monolithic withdrawal from the body into the life of the mind runs counter to the concrete and pluralistic kind of life of real affection and commitment that is expressive of a redemptive concern for the world. The oft-stated view that by withdrawing from an "exclusive relationship" with one person, one is freeing oneself to love and be the father of everyone rests on a very peculiar view of the psychology of human relationships. Its "exclusivity" is that of the private property relationship of the male over the female in the sexual relationship, and not that of real interpersonality. Further, it ignores the fact that no one can love people "in general." One loves and serves people only in real and concrete situations and commitments. In this sense the ethic of withdrawal and non-commitment has created bad theology and bad models of ministry for the Church.

There is, to be sure, still an ethic of risk and insecurity that is relevant to an idea of radical prophetic witness. This has a place in an ethic of messianic hope. But this ethic is aborted when it is institutionalized as a childless, loveless, uncommitted state. The very meaning of an ethic of risk means that one has real loves and ties which are risked. One does indeed have a spouse and child, but lives with these with a provisionality that knows that, sometimes, one must throw up that comforting and nurturing context of daily life in order to witness to the crisis between man's ways and God's demands. In this respect the total security system represented by clerical or monastic life is no more conducive to such a disruption of the routine and the securities of daily life than marriage. Marriage and celibacy both represent institutionalized routines of daily life, and both are disrupted by the real living of a prophetic witness of risk that forces one to break with these security systems.

But, finally, we must see that what has been called an "eschatological ethic," even in the prophetic sense of that term; i.e., radical disaffiliation with institutionalized securities, cannot, by itself, be seen as the whole story of a redemptive, messianic ethic of "building the Kingdom." Redemption is not merely the repudiation of society and creation, but the transformation of society and creation from an alienated, oppressive form to one which can truly become a vehicle of God's presence on earth. The ethic of a faithful "tending of the garden" is as much a part of a redemptive ethic as the occasional need for the breaking of ties and radical disaffiliation with debased social structures. One departs occasionally from the life processes of ordinary society, not in order to reject what is "natural" for the "sake of the Kingdom," but in order to reject what is unnatural and dehumanized in them in order to redeem created life processes to become better vehicles of humanization.

An authentic ethic of the Kingdom must be one that is in continuity with a Biblical view of creation. Within this perspective it seems to me that the pastoral ministry, where life is nurtured in its ordinary life processes, is the normative ministry of the Church, whereas the prophetic ministry of radical disaffiliation with social institutions operates on the transcendent horizon where human society must sometimes make profound breaks with a dehumanized past in order to come again into a renewed vision of the fullness of created life. This latter kind of prophetic ministry cannot really be institutionalized at all. It must rise charismatically, in the "Spirit" and in the context of a particular *kairos*. Moreover, it has nothing in common with institutionalized celibacy. On the other hand, the pastoral ministry is probably expressed normatively, although not necessarily, by those who cultivate the ordinary nutritive processes of life that relate men to women, raise children and build community. The pastoral ministry now, as in the New Testament view, is then normatively a married ministry—however, marriage may have to be redefined to overcome the sexism that has traditionally marred it. That is to say, the pastoral ministry is modeled after those experiences and qualifications that make a person a good lover, parent and builder of familial community.

Chapter 5

Judaism and Christianity:
A Dialogue Refused

Christianity regards itself as a religion founded by Jesus Christ in the first century A.D., while Judaism traces its ancestry back to Moses almost a millennium earlier. Yet both of these two religions, in their classical historical form, should be much more properly regarded as parallel streams of religious development, stemming from that parting of the ways between Palestinian and Hellenistic Judaism after the fall of Jerusalem in 70 A.D. Christianity, inheriting the sectarian, apocalyptic and Greek philosophical aspects of this Jewish development, and founded on the new faith in Jesus as the Christ, became more and more a gentile faith, whereas Judaism repudiated both the apocalyptic and the Hellenistic philosophical developments of the preceding centuries and centered itself on that religion of Torah cultivated by the Pharisees. The classical form of both Judaism and Christianity was shaped by sages and theologians whose systems of thought found their fullest ripening around the fourth century A.D.

The fourth century was the age of the great Christian Fathers of the Church. In the East there were Athanasius, Eusebius, John Chrysostom, Gregory Nyssa, Gregory Nazianzus and Basil the Great. On the Latin side, the Church found equally great minds in Jerome, Ambrose and Augustine, whose theology is still normative for both Protestantism and Catholicism. The fourth century was also the age of the Church councils, where the classical definitions of Trinitarian and Christological doctrine were decided by the whole Church. The fourth century saw the rise and rapid spread of monasticism and ascetic spirituality, as well as the foundations of Christian empire under Constantine and Theodosius. Both its classical political culture and its monastic "counter-culture" were characteristic products of the fourth century.

In Judaism, the fourth century also saw the flowering of its classical tradition, with the sages whose work brought the heritage of oral tradition to its conclusion in the Talmud. The Rabbis, who rescued Jewish national life from the destruction of the national and the religious center of Jewish life of the disastrous Jewish Wars of 66-73 A.D. and 133-136 A.D., had refounded Judaism upon the new institutional center in the synagogue and upon the daily observance of the *mizwoth*. In this form, which has been developed by the Pharisees, Judaism was able to surmount what at first appeared to be the decisive blow to the existence of its ancient faith, with the destruction of the temple and the razing of Jerusalem as the capitol of Jewish national life, into which Jews were forbidden even to enter. The religion of the Torah gave birth to the schools of midrashic commentary in Jamnia, Galilee and Babylonia and, from the work of these sages, the Talmudic tradition found completed form, with the Jerusalem Talmud of the fourth century and the Babylonian Talmud of the fifth century. Thus the period of the great Christian Church Fathers paralleled the great age of Talmudic sages in Babylonia; Rabbah bar Nachmani, and Joseph bar Hama, and their pupil Abaye; Raba bar Joseph bar Hama, Nahmani bar Issac, Papa who founded the school at Neres near Sura and Ashi who taught at Sura.[1]

The style and form these rabbinic stages were giving Judaism in Palestine and on the banks of the Tygris differed most strikingly from what was becoming the style of classical Christianity within the Roman empire, newly converted to the religion of Christ. Although both religions claimed to be founded on the identical foundations, in the Scriptures of Moses and the prophets, the religion that saw this as its "Old Testament," fulfilled in Christ, was carrying this in a direction almost diametrically opposite to that development of the tradition taking place among the rabbis. It is the purpose of this essay to analyze, in what can be only the most introductory way, some of these differences. Thereby we hope to suggest some of the critical losses that Christianity sustained because of its dogmatic insistence on its superiority to Judaism, making authentic dialogue between the two impossible after the alienation of the Church from the Synagogue since the first century A.D.

Christianity, by the fourth century, was becoming more and more hieratic, hierarchical and cultic in form. Originally Christianity, like Rabbinic Judaism, had a lay leadership (in contrast to the old temple priesthood). It centered on the communal Scriptural service led by the elders (laymen), and on the breaking of bread in the messianic fellowship meal that took place in the intimate gathering of Christians in an ordinary home. But these simple and non-cultic rites, by the fourth century, had been elaborated into a formal cult that took on all the trappings of a public temple ritual, clothed in the garments of a new temple priesthood and of the royal Roman court, and demanding both a cultic sacerdotal class and magnificent public buildings to celebrate the "Christian mysteries." The Christian ministry was thus becoming a priestly caste. Its leadership was originally chosen from among the members of the local community. Elevation to leadership required no separation of life style from the other members of the community. But gradually the word "elder" came to be interpreted as "priest," in a cultic sense, and "priests" were rigidly separated from the "people," who were now seen as lacking these cultic powers. The priesthood, gaining the privileges of the ancient Roman priesthood from Constantine, was separated in dress, life style and theological understanding from the "laity." This clerical caste itself became increasingly hierarchical. From the president of the local community (the meaning of the word "bishop" in the New Testament), the bishop came

to be seen as the head of a group of communities within a
metropolis, and new levels of authority blossomed above this
office of local bishops; such as metropolitans, episcopal heads
of provinces, dioceses (a political unit in the Roman empire),
and finally those great patriarchs of the capital cities of Alex-
andria, Antioch, Rome and Constantinople. It was a foregone
conclusion that there would finally be a contest between the
patriarchs of Old Rome and New Rome or Constantinople
as to which was the leader of the "whole Church," paralleling
the almost divine figures of the dual emperors of these two
cities of the Eastern and Western halves of the empire.[2] Despite all the ink that has been spilled over the priority of the
"Petrine See," it should be clear that the real determining factor in this argument was the political priority of the city of
Rome within the political culture of the Roman empire. The
Greek Orthodox Church has always been more frank to admit
this, and has argued that the importance of the ancient patri-
archical sees rests not primarily on some presumed apostolic
grounds, but on the historic position of these cities as the
Church incarnated itself into the social structure of the empire.

In contrast to this development of a hierarchical leadership
caste in Christianity, paralleling the imperial social structure,
Judaism remained non-sacerdotal. With the loss of the temple
and the dwindling of the authority of the ancient priestly and
aristocratic class, the rabbinate and the synagogue leadership
was lay. The rabbi was set apart from the community in no
other way than by being a scholar. But the scholarship he cultivated was not esoteric, but a learning which he sought to teach
the whole community. Each member of the community was
expected to imbibe this same learning as much as he could.
The synagogue itself was not a new temple, but a community
center and school that was essentially non-cultic. All the male
members of the community went there to learn and to pray.
Prayer in the traditional synagogue was startlingly individualistic, despite congregational forms that included the whole community. The popular control of the synagogue meant that the
community often ignored some of the stricter dictates of the
rabbis. Thus, for example, although the rabbis succeeded in

excluding Jewish Christians from *leadership* in the synagogue, their diatribes against the *minim* evidently did not succeed in excluding Jewish Christians from the ordinary congregation where they continued to be accepted into the fourth and fifth centuries.[3] Thus where Christianity was becoming cultic, hierarchical and centralized, Judaism was becoming decentralized, non-cultic and democratic, lacking a distinction between priesthood and people.

Christianity in the fourth century was caught up in an extreme ascetical spirituality. The monk who fasted to the point of death, who removed himself from all contact with sexuality, women, family life and even the ordinary amenities of health and hygiene, was becoming the ideal of holiness. To withdraw from the world, not only in the sense of abandoning culture (for the monk originally was no friend of secular classical learning), all concern with economic, political or social life, and even a rigid repudiation of the goodness of the body that prized the strange hope of being able to live "as though not in the body," i.e., the "angelic life"; this was the ideal which inspired the leaders of fourth and fifth century Christianity. This dualistic spirituality created that peculiar negativity in Patristic Christianity, not only toward sexuality, but even toward the family, the goodness of children and reproduction *per se*. Eating, washing, aesthetic feeling, all that was related to the senses became suspect.

Originally Christianity, like the Jewish synagogue, modeled its religious community after the family. In the Pastoral Epistles of the New Testament, the qualifications for the Christian ministry are seen as identical with those traits that make for a good husband, father and trustworthy family man. But, by the fourth century, ascetic spirituality was removing the Christian ministry from normal contact with family life. Marriage was seen as preventing the priest from achieving that purity and total devotion to God necessary for one who offers a pure sacrifice. All contact with sex was seen as intrinsically polluting and distracting.[4] An ascetic and cultic concept of "purity" was making celibacy mandatory for the priesthood, although it would be many centuries before this was really enforced among the parish priests in the Western Church and it never became regular for the Eastern Church. Nevertheless, marriage was seen as a "lower" state of life. Priests who were married were expected to put away sexual contact with their wives. Even for the ordinary Christian, marriage was seen as the choice of those who lack the full grace of conversion to the resurrected life of Christ.

Rabbinic Judaism presents a diametrically opposite picture on this evaluation of sex and family life. Although the rabbis did not lack some of that paranoia which viewed women as an irresistible sexual threat,[5] their remedy for this was marriage and family life, not virginity. Far from despising sexuality, the rabbis even declared that, since the destruction of the temple, the presence of God existed in two places: in the rabbinic houses of study, and when a man lies beside his wife. Judaism was a religion centered on the home and family. The practice of virtue stood in the context of the ordinary social, economic, and political life of the community. There was no ascetic spirituality that made life apart from society one of higher holiness. Even rabbinic learning equipped one to practice virtue in the home and society, and did not remove one from society. Children were always seen as God's highest blessings. But Rabbinic Judaism saw every detail of the physical, created universe as a divine gift to be greeted with constant expressions of thanksgiving (the Jewish root of the word "Eucharist," i.e., to give thanks). The blessings in the Daily Prayer Book, far from forbidding an enjoyment of creation, authorize numerous *berakoth* because "it is a reasonable supposition that it is forbidden a man to enjoy anything in this world without saying a blessing." [6] Blessings were provided for occasions such as eating and drinking, upon seeing a wise man, smelling a perfume, seeing a fruit tree in blossom or experiencing the beauties of nature. In contrast to the Christian separation of the spiritual and the sensual, Judaism was saturating the sensual with spiritual meaning and making every occasion of experiencing the gifts of hand, eye, ear or taste one in which to give thanks to its Creator. Humanness and not the "angelic life" was the ethical norm of a spirituality based on the grace of creation. The use of the term "worldliness" in the two sister faiths illustrate graphically the difference in spiritualities. In Christianity "worldliness" retained its apocalyptic, gnostic sense of all that was "evil," but this came to be identified with the natural physical creation itself. The "carnal" was that which was evil and debased. For Judaism, on the other hand, the term *derek eretz,* i.e., the way of the world, stood as the criterion for what is proper and in accordance with the integrity of human nature as a part of God's creation.

Perhaps the difference in concepts of hygiene illustrates the gulf between the spiritualities of the two religions that had developed. In ascetical Christianity the cultivation of dirt, the neglect of the cleanliness of clothes and the body, symbolized a disregard for the well-being of the flesh. Such extolling of "squalor," as one finds in St. Jerome and other fourth century monks would have been incomprehensible to Judaism, which laid down the most minute rules for health and cleanliness. For Judaism, hygiene was a religious duty. This had the side effect of making for more hygienic conditions in the ghetto within medieval Christian cities that often preserved them from the plagues that swept the filth-ridden Christian sectors. It is ironic to realize that this fact also helped at that time to generate the paranoid Christian myth that the Jews were responsible for these plagues which swept the Christian sector but left the Jewish ghetto untouched! The traditional Jewish cultivation of the medical profession was also a side benefit of these practices, so that medieval Christians, while often superstitiously attributing diabolical magical powers to Jews, nevertheless called on them for medical help.[7] The king's doctor was frequently a Jew.

Judaism was centered on conformity to God's will in the here and now. Eschatological reward was not discounted, but its spirituality was centered on the fulfillment of creation rather than on an eschatology which thrust man beyond the framework of historical existence. This has been generally misunderstood by that Christian theology which followed St. Paul in his hostile view of the Torah as a "salvation by works." The whole framework of Paul's interpretation of the Torah as "justification by works" is unacceptable to a Judaism which believes neither in Original Sin nor in "justification," in the

Pauline sense. For Judaism, faith cannot be separated from deed, nor grace from nature. Thus the dualism of grace and the law is fundamentally unacceptable. The spirituality of the Torah (which properly means "the Way," rather than "the law," a misunderstanding that came into Christianity through the Greek translation of Torah as *nomos* in the Septuagint) is aimed at the hallowing of life here and now in obedience to God's commandments. Its spirituality is, then, self-contained and self-fulfilling. The legal and the mystical intertwine in a way of life in which the most minute act of obedience to God's will becomes an occasion for experiencing the drawing near of God's *Skekhinah*. It is this living in the presence of God that is the purpose of the whole practice of Torah, and this view has given birth to sects such as the Hasidim in seventeenth century Poland, where the practice of Torah itself becomes ecstatic, mystical and jubilant with song and dance. To see the rabbi dancing through the synagogue with the Torah in his arms is to suspect a view of Torah that has little to do with the Christian concept of Judaism as a deadening "legalism."

The Christian emphasis upon the dualities of body and soul, the secular and the sacred, the Church and the world, and even this world and the next, are foreign to Jewish thinking. The hope for the messianic age remains, but it continues to be held as a future horizon of history, so much so that the Exilarch of Babylonia, by reason of his Davidic descent, can reasonably put forth his claim to be a messianic figure, while the rabbis dispute with him on the grounds that the messianic age is brought about through observance of the Torah, and not merely by political peace and security.[8] The word "heaven" then is not so much a place that one goes to by abandoning the earth, as that place of God's presence which one seeks to bring near by hallowing daily life. The messianic age will be that time when this hallowing of created life in the presence of God will be fulfilled in its fullest, i.e., when "God's will is done on earth, as it is in heaven." Thus daily life is not lived in a spirituality that abstracts man from creation, the body and society, but rather seeks to draw God's holy presence into these forms of daily life, so that every aspect of ordinary activities becomes a prayer and God's *Skekhinah* comes near and hallows the earth.

Where Christianity in this period degraded sexuality, the body and even the goodness of children, seeing even offspring of legitimate unions as a doubtful blessing best dispensed with by those who would live in the new order of the resurrection from the dead, the blessings of children continued to be seen in Judaism as God's highest gift. Strange indeed in Jewish ears would have been that Christian doctrine that the defiling character of sex so tainted the child with an hereditary sinfulness that it became the means for the transmission of Original Sin. For Jews, man has indeed good and bad tendencies, but he was free and responsible to choose between them. Adam's fall was not treated as an Original Sin that fundamentally removed man's capacity for good. Indeed, Christians should seriously ask themselves whether this doctrine in St. Paul was not more gnostic than Jewish.

Judaism also knew no such separation of the sacred and the secular, the religious from the social community. In this sense the Jew had no "church," because his ordinary social community was his religious community. With the loss of the temple, Judaism even dispensed with a sacral cultic center, for the synagogue was not a temple in that traditional sense. Rather it was the home that became the center of Judaism's liturgical life. The home is the place where the High Holidays are celebrated, and the liturgies of the great festivals were designed to be celebrated around the family dinner table. Here too woman, often scorned and derided by the rabbis for her lack of (exclusion from) learning, had her special dignity, for the mother was the minister of the religious observances of the home in many ways; presiding over the ritual preparation of food, and the blessing of the fire that started every family celebration. The home, therefore, was the "church," in the sense of cultic or liturgical center, whereas the synagogue was primarily a community center of learning, prayer and social life, as much school as house of prayer, lacking any cultic priesthood.

In theological style Judaism also took a widely different

form from its sister religion to the West. Christianity developed as a doctrinal religion, borrowing the categories of Greek philosophy to develop great dogmatic systems that were hammered out with precise definitional formulas. This doctrinal character of Christianity lent itself to that *odium theologicum* that became characteristic of Patristic theological discussions. Factionalism and murderous disputatiousness filled the air of fourth century Christianity, as proponents of different doctrinal definitions anathematized each other and appealed to the emperor to punish their opponents. Ironically enough, Christians regarded the Jews as having been cursed by God for failing to accept Jesus as the Christ, and punished through the loss of political power and their national homeland. Yet Judaism, in fourth century Iran, was reaping the benefits of a relative security and detachment from political power, that left it free to cultivate standards of conduct within its local communities. Christianity, by contrast, was experiencing all the disadvantages of becoming identified with the Roman empire as its imperial religion. This identification turned every consideration of doctrine into a question of political favor within the framework of Roman imperial power. Heresy, then, placed a man not only outside the pale of Church fellowship, but outside legal and civic rights as well. Christianity, which only a short time before had pleaded for toleration under persecution, within fifty years of its establishment as the religion of the empire had become the persecutor of every other form of religious expression. Not only Judaism and all forms of non-Biblical religion, but every stripe of dissident Christianity became subject to laws that excluded their adherents from the rights of legal existence, worship, participation in government and even ordinary livelihood. Heresy became a crime punishable by banishment or death, although for a time the traditional protection accorded the Jews as an ethnic minority under the laws of the earlier pagan government protected Judaism from the zealousness of the laws which orthodox Christianity was now passing against heresy and paganism(!).[9] Nevertheless, by the fifth century Judaism found itself subject to synagogue burnings and forced baptisms by

Christian mobs, often led by fanatical monks, and was being forced down the road, legally and socially, to that position of marginal existence without guaranteed legal rights that was to be its position in Medieval Christendom, until the Enlightenment. The kind of change that had taken place within the traditional Roman government's view of protection of minorities is witnessed to in the famous incident between Theodosius and St. Ambrose. When a crowd of fanatical Christians burned a synagogue in Asia Minor, the emperor ordered the Christian community in that area to rebuild it. Ambrose, incensed that any funds from the Church should be used to build a synagogue, ordered the emperor excommunicated until he rescinded his order, and finally was able to force him to do so.[10] In the eight sermons which John Chrysostom preached against the Jews at festival times, c. 386-7 A.D., the development from the exegetical polemics of earlier Christian literature "Against the Jews" to the tone of unrestrained diabolizing has already been struck. In these sermons the synagogue is endlessly denounced as a "hotel of demons"; a place filled with every evil, and even the souls of Jews are said to be inhabited by devils.[11] It is perhaps not unimportant to note that the reason for the preaching of these sermons was the fact that so many Christians in Antioch continued to frequent the synagogue and observe Jewish practices, fasts and festivals. It seems that the ordinary Christians had not yet learned the message of hatred which the religious virtuosi were trying to teach them!

In this period Judaism had abandoned that amalgamation with Greek philosophy which some exegetes of the Hellenistic school had tried to insert into its framework in the first century. It is often said that Judaism is orthopractic rather than orthodox. It centers on a comprehensive code of practices aimed at sanctifying every aspect of daily life, rather than on credal definition. The touchstone for the development of Torah-practice, however, was that nothing should be legislated that could not be borne by the whole community. Indeed, there is good evidence that the rabbis had no means of forcing upon the community those things which the community itself did not wish to accept or regarded as too burdensome.[12] The rabbis were not concerned about "endless multiple regulations," as Christians often believe, but were practical community leaders, who used the means of oral tradition to alter or abolish those laws that had become obsolete. The rabbinic insistence that Israel was meant to "live in the commandments; not to die in them," allowed considerable flexibility in adapting the *mizwoth* to circumstances.[13] Judaism, moreover, continued to welcome converts, despite increasingly vehement laws passed by Christian governments against conversion to Judaism or even social contact between Christian and Jew. The rabbis, in turn, also made vehement statements against social contact with Christians and those of other religions, but, in practice, this was largely ignored by the Jewish community, and even rabbis clearly had social fellowship with those of other religions in their own homes.[14] The crucial difference here was the political power of the Christian leadership to enforce its position, and the lack of the same on the Jewish side. Judaism was ethnocentric, but it was Christianity, not Judaism, that created the ghetto.

Talmudic commentary does not represent so much the search to abstract doctrine from the Scriptures or even to come to fixed conclusions about the interpretation of practices, so much as it records a process of discussion. It is not a collection of finished "laws" or "doctrines," but the cumulative collective consciousness of a people. This is perhaps what makes reading it so difficult for those of other traditions. It is rather like reading the continuing running notes of a process of discussion made in a free academy over a period of many hundreds of years. Thus the transmission of the tradition never became a means of closing off discussion, but rather an open-ended invitation to each generation to continue the discussion. Judaism, moreover, always protected the minority opinion by giving it a place in the tradition. The form of the tradition usually gives the opinion of two different teachers, representing different schools of commentary, each passed down as authoritative, although the easier and more humane view is seen as preferred.

Since Judaism was based on ethical practice and not on doctrine, its theology remained unsystematic. Its most solemn beliefs were never made the subject of systematic expositions,

but rather occur in an almost folkloric form in the midst of discussion of random details of halakic observance. The mixture
of *halakah* and *haggadah* in Jewish commentary is confusing to
Christian ears, which find the most profound theological
thoughts occuring in quaint folkloric comments in the midst of
what appear to be minutiae of rules and regulations. The style
is frankly anthropomorphic, discursive and even bantering.
God and the rabbis argue and cajole with each other on intimate terms. The voice of God is often used by the rabbis to
rebuke the prejudices of the people, such as the famous *haggadah* on the Exodus story, where the Jewish people are
pictured as dancing and rejoicing while the Egyptians are
drowning in the Red Sea, and the voice of God intervenes
from heaven to demand the cause of their merriment at a time
when "my sons, the Egyptians, are dying." [15] Weighty matters
are sometimes treated lightly and in a way that even sounds, to
those of a different theological style, "undignified." Thus the
rabbis can come to surprising and quixotic conclusions to illustrate values, without necessarily tying themselves down to a
dogmatic implication. For example, one third century Palestinian rabbi could treat the doctrine of future life as so tan-
gential to immediate concerns as to declare that the day of
good rain was more blessed than the day of the Resurrection,
because the day of the Resurrection benefited only the righteous, whereas the day of a good rain benefited sinners and
righteous alike.[16] Such a comment is quite compatible with
rabbinic style and psychology, but one could hardly imagine
such a view in the mouth of a Christian Church Father!

Since the rabbis were, above all, concerned to hold up an
ideal of obedience in the midst of the community, rather than
to separate out of the community in the manner of the monks,
even their own concern with learning and strict practice could
be modified by their sense of communal solidarity. The stress
on righteousness found its constant compliment in the stress
upon mercy and the virtues of loving-kindness as the highest
value. This view is charmingly expressed in the famous midrashic commentary on the meaning of the *lulav;* the nosegay
of citron, palm, myrtle and willow that was waved during the
Feast of Tabernacles. According to this commentary, the citron,

which has both taste and fragrance, stands for those in Israel who have both learning and good deeds. The palm, which has taste but no fragrance, stands for those who have learning, but no good deeds. The myrtle, which has fragrance, but no taste, stands for those who have good deeds, but no learning. The willow stands for those thick twigs of Israel who have neither learning nor good deeds. "What then does the Holy One, Blessed be He, do with them? To destroy them is impossible. But, says the Holy One, blessed be He, let them all be tied together in one band, and they will all atone, one for another. If you have done so, (says the Lord), then, at that instant I am exalted." [17]

The comparison of the literatures of classical Christianity and Talmudic Judaism at first seems to weigh heavily against the latter. Christianity thought in those systematic forms that proceeded through the formal structure of a doctrine from beginning to end. However much modern Western man may disagree with its presuppositions, the form of Christianity is the form familiar to him as the basis of formal philosophical presentation. Classical Judaism, although it also had its own forms of logical reasoning, produced a literature which looks, at first sight, like someone's grandmother's attic where endless quantities of curious things which "someday might come in handy" have been passed down like so many balls of string lovingly collected over the years and piled on top of each other without concern for distinctions of (what Christians might think are) weighty and trival matters; i.e., doctrine, as distinct from details of daily life. But this judgment springs from an entirely different sense of ordering from that which governed the formation of the Talmud. It is only with the greatest difficulty that those accustomed to systematic modes of ordering, in a doctrinal framework, can begin to adjust themselves to the discursive style of the rabbis and begin to discern the quite different way of weighing the weighty and the trivial that guides their discussions and linking of theme to theme. But gradually it becomes clear that this apparent jumble of piety and details of ordinary life is the very medium of the rabbinic message, which is the effort to penetrate every corner of ordinary life with the sense of God's presence. This expressed itself in an innocence of the classical hierarchies of being and value, while finding nothing incongruous at all about making the most profound comments on the nature of God in the midst of discussing the relative uses of cheese.

The difference in value orientation and also the difference in political power were generating a very considerable difference in actual life style between these two faiths which parted ways after the fall of Jerusalem and thereafter fell into increasing estrangement, so that even the word "Jew," in the mouths of the Church Fathers, takes on the character of a curse. Christianity thinks of itself as the religion of grace and forgiveness, and likes to use the word "Christian" as synonymous with "love." Yet, by the fourth century, it had become a religion characterized far more by intolerance of differences among its own ranks, by hierarchical and imperious forms of life, and by an inhuman spirituality that was matched by an increasing willingness to invoke the arm of the state to punish religious dissent. Since it was the imperial religion, it felt qualified to extend its judgment against pagans and Jews, as well as heretics, and to purge out of the state all those who did not adhere to orthodox Christianity. Judaism, by contrast, typically ignored as outside its jurisdiction those who were not Jews, including Christians. Its strictures against Christians, therefore, were from the beginning limited to Jewish Christians, and even these, contrary to a general misunderstanding even among scholars, were not excluded from the synagogue, but only from leading the synagogue service.[18] In the fourth and fifth centuries Christian mobs burned synagogues, sacked ancient temples and libraries and walled the priests of rival religions, such as Mithraism, into their sanctuaries to die.[19] Even Augustine, the theologian of grace, used the text Luke 14: 23, that spoke of going out into the highways and byways to bring in the poor, the lame and the halt into the messianic banquet, to justify the use of legal force and persecution against religious dissenters, such as the native African Donatist Church.[20]

The religion of Torah, in this same period, asked only for the peace and security to spin its silken threads of learning in its own community. It largely won this peace beyond the borders of the Christian empire in Babylonia. There it was creating a life style in which every detail of reality could be seen as penetrated by God's Spirit. Hillel, in the first century, had already laid down the precept that the whole Law is contained in the commandment that we should not do to our brothers what is hateful to us.[21] The rabbis argued that prayer and obedience to the commandments had replaced burnt offerings of the temple, as the more acceptable sacrifice to God. Through this way of life the messianic age would come to the people.[22] The rabbis interpreted the word for justice, *zedekah,* so that it became synonymous with "loving-kindness" [23] and argued that therein was contained the highest fulfillment of the works of the Law. It is not surprising, then, that Jews have ever felt impatient with the Christian argument that Christianity replaced the sacrifice of burnt offerings with the spiritual sacrifice of prayer and the contrite heart and changed the Law from one of retribution to the law of love, for both of these principles were characteristic of Rabbinic Judaism in this same period. Christianity, by contrast, gave no such convincing proof of being, in reality, that superior religion of love.

The rabbis argued that deeds of loving-kindness were superior to deeds of monetary charity, because these demand only one's physical means, whereas deeds of loving-kindness demand the giving of one's whole person and can benefit rich and poor alike.[24] Since Judaism was a religious community, rather than a "church," its laws made no distinction between religious and social duties. All one's ordinary social duties were also duties to be passed under that ethical scrutiny of obedience to God. Thus the distinction typical of Christianity of religious and social life did not occur in Judaism, and this altered considerably its standards of daily life. The standards of life in rabbinic law courts compare favorably with the most enlightened legislation produced by the modern system of jurisprudence. Compared with standards reigning at the same time in classical and medieval Christendom, the contrast is considerable. For example, torture, common in Christian courts, was unknown in rabbinic courts. There was no class above the law or privileged within the law. Much of the emphasis was directed to the special protection of the poor, the weak and the dispossessed Even animals had rights under Jewish law.[25]

The weaknesses of an ingrown character of Judaism that would appear as a consequence of a thousand years of persecution in the Christian ghettos of Europe had not yet appeared, and many of the strengths of Judaism in the period are remarkable in their ability to complement those aspects where Christianity was becoming gnostic in spirituality and blunted in its sense of community. Yet the very possibility that Christianity could have learned some of these things through a continued interaction with Judaism was entirely ruled out and is still ruled out for most Christians today through the dogmatic insistence that Judaism was an obsolete and retrograde religion that had been superceded by the Christian gospel "of love." This dogmatic insistence on the superiority of Christianity and the rejected character of Judaism, moreover, increasingly took the form of having, visibly, to prove this proposition by thrusting Jews into legal ghettos within Christian societies (and ultimately into extermination camps). Since the sixteenth century, Christianity has been going through continual upheavals against the classical dogmatic, ascetic and sacerdotal forms that were developed in the Patristic period. The development even of Catholic Christianity today is toward a self-modification that aims at democraticizing it, de-culticizing it, removing the ascetic and sacerdotal character of its ministry, to make them more leaders within and of the community, and to make its spirituality more humane, tolerant, this-worldly and life-affirming. Yet most Christians even today have so imbibed the doctrine of the spiritual superiority of Christianity that they find it almost impossible to imagine that they might find in this sister faith, that was writing its Talmud at the same time as the great Church councils, an ally and resource for the development of those very characteristics that it has lacked and which, more and more, it wishes to claim for itself. Perhaps most important, as its central doctrine of Christology falls more and more into doubt, it may find the assistance of Judaism imperative to rediscover all over again what the word "Messiah" really means in the Scriptures.

A little story may illustrate the conditions under which the possibility of dialogue between Judaism and Christianity failed in the classical period. In sixth century Syria, Babylonia and Egypt, dialogue between Christians and Jews in set disputations was not uncommon, if we can judge from the literature. But seldom in this literature are the Jews allowed to appear as more than straw men for the Christian position. However, occasionally in unconscious ways, the real character of the Jewish query to Christianity is allowed to creep in, if in no other way than in the final resolution of the discussion through miraculous intervention from heaven, rather than through argument. In one of these disputations, *The Trophies of Damascus,* the Jewish questioners argue that the Messiah cannot have come already, because the messianic peace, which was promised as the sign of his coming, has not yet appeared. The Christian monk, at first, insists that this peace referred solely to inward or spiritual peace and so does not pertain to real transformation of the world. Then, as if dissatisfied with such a feeble effect of the messianic advent in Christian society, the monk argues that, indeed, the Byzantine empire had enjoyed peace until fifty years ago (!). Finally he asserts evasively that God sometimes says one thing and does another. But the Christian "God" in these discussions increasingly shows an alarming propensity to dispense with argument altogether, by intervening with thunderclaps and intimidating visions to force the Jews into submission, silence or forced baptism.[26] At this point the possibility of discussion ended between Judaism and Christianity, to be opened again only after the holocaust suggested to some Christians that this whole history might have contained a fundamental flaw.

NOTES

1. Jacob Neusner, *A History of the Jews in Babylonia* (Leiden: Brill, 1965-6), vols. 3 and 4.

2. H. R. Niebuhr and D. Williams, *The Ministry in Historical Perspective* (N.Y.: Harpers, 1956), chapters, 1 and 2.

3. *b. Ber.* 33b; Jacob Neusner, *Torah and Synagogue* (N.Y., 1965), pp. 96-97.

4. William Phipps, *Was Jesus Married? The Distortion of Sexuality in the Christian Tradition* (N.Y.: Harpers, 1970), pp. 75-98.

5. Neusner, *A History of the Jews in Babylonia,* vol. 3, pp. 142-45 and pp. 276ff.

6. *Berakoth,* ch. 6, 35a ff., p. 220; see James Parkes, *The Foundations of Judaism and Christianity* (Chicago: Quadrangle, 1960), p. 291.

7. Joshua Trachtenberg, *The Devil and the Jews* (Yale University Press, 1943).

8. Neusner, *A History of the Jews in Babylonia,* vol. 3, pp. 62ff.; also Neusner, "Rabbis and Community in Third-Century Babylonia," in J. Neusner, ed., *Religions in Antiquity; Essays in Memory of Erwin Ramsdell Goodenough* (Leiden: Brill, 1967), pp. 438-62.

9. James Parkes, *The Conflicts of Church and Synagogue* (N.Y.: Meridian, 1961), chapters 6, 7 and pp. 177-82; see also S. L. Greenslade, *Church and State from Constantine to Theodosius* (London: SCM Pr., 1954).

10. Ambrose, *Epp.* 40 and 41: see F. H. Dudden, *The Life and Times of St. Ambrose* (Oxford: Clarendon Press, 1935), vol. II, pp. 371-380.

11. J. Chrysostom, *Adversos Judaeos;* Orationes 8; Migne, *P.G.,* vol. 48, pp. 843-942.

12. Neusner, "Rabbis and Community in Third Century Babylonia," *op. cit.*

13. *San.* 74a, p. 502; Parkes, *Foundations,* pp. 288-9.

14. Neusner, *A History of the Jews in Babylonia,* vol. 4, pp. 56-72.

15. Cited in Samuel Sandmel, *We Jews and You Christians* (N.Y.: Lippincott, 1967), p. 20.

16. *Ta'an* 7a, p. 24.

17. *Lev.* 23, 43 in *Midrash Rabba* on Leviticus 30, 12.

18. This is the conclusion of D. R. A. Hare, in his study of the laws of the exclusion of Christians from the synagogue, relative to the Gospel of Matthew; *The Theme of Jewish Persecution of Christians in the Gospel According to Matthew* (Cambridge University Press, 1967); Neusner's remarks on the relations between Jews and Christians in Babylonia from the third to the seventh centuries also indicates that Christians were not excluded from the synagogue in practice, but only from leading the service: *op. cit.,* note 1, above.

19. On Christian persecutions of Mithraism, see Franz Cumont, *The Mysteries of Mithra* (N.Y.: Dover, 1956), pp. 203-206.

20. Augustine, *Epistle* 93.2.5; See W. H. C. Frend, *The Donatist Church* (Oxford, 1953), p. 241.

21. *Shab.* 31a, p. 140.

22. Neusner, *A History of the Jews in Babylonia,* vol. 5, p. 212ff.

23. Max Kadushen, *Organic Thinking* (Jerusalem: 1938), pp. 219ff; see Parkes, *Foundations,* p. 297.

24. *Suk.* 49b, p. 233; see Parkes, *ibid.,* p. 298.

25. J. J. Rabmowitz, *Jewish Law; Its Influence on the Development of Legal Institutions* (N.Y.: 1956), chapter 5; also Parkes, *Foundations,* pp. 308-317.

26. Parkes, *Church and Synagogue, op. cit.,* pp. 276-290.

Chapter 6

Christian Anti-Semitism and the Dilemma of Zionism

"The Jew is the Achilles heel of Christianity," Albert Memmi, the French Tunisian Jew, quotes Manes Sperber as saying, in Memmi's classical study, *The Liberation of the Jew*. The refusal of the Jewish people to accept the fulfillment of their messianic hope in Christianity remains the visible sign of Christianity's questionableness; the living contradiction of its claim to be the heir of the messianic hope of that people whose Scriptures it ideologically calls the "Old Testament." This living contradiction furnished by the continued existence of Judaism has, from the beginnings of Christianity to the present, called forth from Christianity various elaborations of a particular theological explanation. The Jew was identified as the man "of the letter," in contrast to the Christian in whom the letter was fulfilled "in the Spirit." Judaism was defined by the Church Fathers as the "carnal image" of what had been fulfilled by Christ on a higher level, surpassing Judaism spiritually and historically. The Jew was thus left with only an empty shell of an obsolete religion which had existed only to point beyond itself. The "Old Testament" prophets were read out of context by Christian exegetes in such a way as to dismember the prophetic dialectic between judgment and promise. All sin and judgment were identified as the lineage of the Jew, while the Church inherited the lineage of the Promise. In this way the Church Fathers constructed a portrait of the Jew of unrelieved perversity, to which his ultimate rejection by God and replacement by the Church was the appropriate retribution. The refusal of the Jews to regard this as an appropriate judgment on their religion or to find in a Jesus served up to them on these terms the Messiah of Jewish hope was seen by the Church as simply the ongoing expression of this same historic perversity and moral blindness that is the Jew. The spiritual identity of the Jew thus became reified in Christian theology as the inveterately "graceless man" who can only know "after the flesh." This theological portrait of the Jew continues on from the "New Testament" and Church Fathers to Barth.

The result of this theological portrait, translated into sociological relationships between a dominant Christian society and a scattered Jewry, was to draw a total ghetto around the traditional particularism of the Jewish community. All options for existence for the Jew were defined by reference to this negative Christian portrait. As Memmi describes it so brilliantly in his study of the dilemma of the Jew, the Jew was trapped on every side by this negative condition imposed on him from without, despite his internal rejection of it. Did the Jew wish to affirm himself in his Jewishness? What then could he affirm except a ghettoized culture that existed simply as an internal portrait of this negative condition? Would the Jew break out of this ghetto and affirm himself simply as a man? Every way out of the ghetto within Christian society turned out to be simply another version of the Christian demand that the Jew be "saved" by ceasing to exist as a Jew. Whether it be the pogrom or the cultural death of conversion or assimilation, the demise of the Jew was the presupposition of a totalized Christian identity. Christianity, as the fulfilled universalism of a particularism, could not tolerate the continued contrary particularism of the Jew.

In the nineteenth century, as Christendom was forced to retreat before secularism, the Jew found a new option for emergence from the ghetto into a common humanity no longer defined by Christian anti-Semitism. With explosive force, this long pent-up people emerged as leaders in a variety of cultural and social endeavors. The price they paid was self-rejection of their own religious identity, which must remain behind them in the ghetto; the effort to stand as "secular Jews" in the midst of secular Christians in a common secular nationality. But this option quickly betrayed them. Christian anti-Semitism was not overcome, but merely translated into a secular language. The new prominence of the Jew reawakened the view of the Jew as a mysteriously malignant and conspiratorial threat, so long cultivated by Christianity. No matter how he protested his secularity or even sought to conceal his Jewishness under a variety of strategems, the Jew was sniffed out and his accomplishments felt as an affront to the identity of the dominant culture.

Many Jews sought to relieve this tension by fleeing into the Movement for universal human liberation. Here was the secular equivalent of Jewish messianic hope. But the Revolution, too, betrayed the Jew. The prominence of a few Jews in the Left was interpreted by the Christian, ecclesiastical Right as the quintessence of that malignancy of "modern materialism" manifest in "godless Communism." The very sanctuary of secularity among Jews of the Left only confirmed the ecclesiastical Right in its identification of the Jew as the eternal moving spirit in the ranks of the "enemies of God." But the Left, in turn, in Marxism, defined the Jew as the typical "capitalist" or "bourgeois." Thus the success of the Revolution demanded of the Leftist Jew an assent to his own self-annihilation. The Jew of the Left must prove his socialist credentials by being more militantly anti-Semitic than his own enemies! Even when he made this sacrifice of himself for the sake of the Revolution, the Jew found he had been tricked in his quest for comrades in the Revolution. After the Revolution, Marxist anti-Semitism united with the unreformed anti-Semitism of the post-Christian masses of socialist countries to sniff out the Jew in the party ranks as the "revisionist"; the covert bourgeois; the secret enemy of the Revolution, whose very continuance in his particularity was an affront to the victory of the "classless society." The Jew thus found that, in endorsing the Revolution, he had endorsed a secular equivalent of the same kind of fulfilled messianism which, in Christianity, had demanded the disappearance of the Jew as the price of its own totalization.

It was the recognition of the inescapability of this trap, it seems to me, that created that pervasive *sadness* of a Jew such as I knew in my own uncle. Like many Jews of that generation, my uncle and his brothers had abandoned their religious roots with the secular liberation demanded by departure from the ghetto. Their Jewishness was a kind of inexplicable fact of their historical situation which had lost its interpretive key. For them, the synagogue and its traditions were a closed book; a collection of obsolete and soul-constricting gestures which had lost all life-giving power. They could hardly imagine what it meant to be Jewish in a religious sense. And yet assimilation also was failing them. Having lost their roots, they were still Jewish withal; still despised withal; although neither side could quite recall the original reasons. My uncle's desperate efforts to be baptized at the instructions of Msgr. Fulton Sheen ended in a terrified retreat back into his Jewishness that could no more deny itself than it could find its own meaning. An enormously talented man in art and music, with a voice worthy of an operatic star, he lived all his life in a state bordering on suicidal self-doubt (indeed his father had committed suicide) that made it impossible for him to actualize his talents in any significant way, except to impart them as an avuncular gift to his Christian nieces. When his nieces committed the disservice of moving to the other side of the country, the light went out of his eyes and he died inside. The youthful socialist leanings of my uncle and his brothers only confirmed the trap in which they continued to exist in a residually Christian society. As Marxist intellectuals, even of the most dilettantish kind, they found themselves metamorphosed into the latest secular version of the old "Jewish Devil." Meanwhile the Left itself was rapidly proving, in Eastern Europe, its unwillingness to actualize that hope for the liberation of the Jew for which they had hoped when they espoused the cause of the liberation of "all men."

For the Jews of this generation, Memmi among them,

there could only be one alternative to the various kinds of genocide proposed as the "final solution to the Jewish question" within the Christian exile. Liberation must be the disappearance of Judaism into Zionism; a "land of our own" where we can be a true people, with a true nationality and a homeland; where, at last, the Jew can affirm himself without, at the same time, negating himself. For Memmi, indeed, Judaism itself is only a psychopathology expressive in symbolic terms of this alienation from a true national identity and homeland, and will "wither away" once this need is realized. Zionism fused Jewish messianism, particularism and the best dreams of Jewish communitarian socialism, to make of Israel the solution to the Jewish need for liberation. But, unfortunately, this mythical land of promise was no more unoccupied in the twentieth century than when Joshua marched into it three and a half millennia earlier. And so the Jewish claim to the land of Israel, as his particular land of liberation, must be purchased at the expense of the self-determination and existence in that same land by its previous inhabitants. With tragic irony, Israel's liberation became the enemy of Palestinian liberation; the right of the Jewish people to exist became the negation of the right of another oppressed people to exist. This situation is hardly alleviated by new demands of ritual self-sacrifice of Jewish existence by the Left, nor by a Christian philo-Semitism, which, in its guilt, wishes to echo with theological language a God-given right of Jews to this particular piece of the earth. Rather, we must recognize the objective dilemma which the very psychology of the Exile had projected upon its national solution. How could the Jews of the Exile, who had seen the paralysis of every option for liberation within the Diaspora and still had the smell of burning flesh from the holocaust in their nostrils to remind them of its "ultimate solution," be flexible when adjusting the imperative of a place for Jews to exist to that of another crushed and all but unnoticed people?

Arthur Waskow, in his book, *The Bush is Burning* provides a description of the dilemma which the very psychology of the Exile has imposed on Israeli self-definition, and tries to point to a new vision beyond that of Albert Memmi. For Waskow, the solution to Jewish liberation is not merely a dissolution of a religious identity into a nationalist one, especially when that nationalist identity is defined as a projection of the anxiety of the Exile. Rather the Jew must regrasp his religious identity in a way that can define him both as a people and as the bearer of an historical message that must set the Jew in tension with his own failures to liberate himself and to stand for the liberation of all men. The existence of Israel has abolished the Exile, only in the sense of making it necessary to recognize this same tension both within Israel and within communities of Jews in the Diaspora. The anxiety of Jews in the American Diaspora especially, which makes of Israel the symbol of ultimate recourse should the mirage of assimilation fail them too, lines up the Jewish establishment here in solidarity with the most reactionary elements of American imperialism and helps to lock Israeli foreign policy into an inflexible either-or between Al Fatah and Zionism. For Waskow, this means that Israel progressively betrays its inner religious promise to be truly Zion; to become that mountain from which the message of liberation can go forth to all men and "all flesh can see it together." Instead, Israel has become a part of the *galut,* modeled in the obverse image of the *galut* of the Diaspora.

For Israel, Waskow would prescribe the emergence of a binational state modeled on communitarian socialist principles that would give self-determination to each community. But such a development is predicated upon the relaxation of that defensive posture defined by the two terrors of physical annihilation and cultural assimilation. Only when this twin threat is relaxed for Jews throughout the world, can the Jewish establishment begin to imagine the possibility of a Jewish survival not based on exclusive Jewish control of a Jewish state at the expense of the Palestinians. The forces on the Left within Israeli society can be allowed to emerge that could mediate a new option between the present positions of mutual negation. Waskow is suggesting a crucial interdependence between the threatened life of the Jew of the Diaspora and its obverse image in the endlessly self-defensive stance of Israel. For Waskow, only when the Diaspora ceases to be merely *galut* and becomes defined as a place of positive mission and community for the Jew, can the American Jewish establishment relax its stranglehold on Israeli national policy, which now lines them up with American imperialism and lays the basis for a new rationale for anti-Semitism on the Left.

What would be the conditions for such a liberated Judaism in the Diaspora, no longer merely trapped between the twin dangers of genocide and assimilation? Waskow sees the key to this in a non-Marxist communitarian socialism which unites radical social change with Jewish prophetism in a context which is both universalistic and yet specific to the role and identity of each historical community. Only in this way can the modern Jew reaffirm the saying of the ancient Jewish sage: "If I am not for myself, who will be for me? but if I am for myself alone, what kind of a man am I?" No longer must he sacrifice his Jewishness on the altar of an abstract universalism of the Old Left, nor his universalism for his national survival, as has become the fate of present Israel. Waskow sees in this option a revivification of the riches of the Jewish tradition, which never separated religion from life, the individual from the community or man from nature. Talmudic wisdom thus coincides in a new way with a post-technological, ecological and communitarian vision of liberation. The particularism of the Jewish tradition coincided with, rather than contradicted, its universalism, and allowed a contextual view of each nation under God that gave each its path, in solidarity rather than competition with the identity of the other. Communitarian socialism allows the affirmation of this contextualism, which is the authentic way of understanding Jewish particularism. Now one does not merely bring judgment against the "Nations," but judges all in the light of God's demand, and, on the other side of judgment, affirms, "Blessed be Egypt, my people, and Assyria, the work of my hands, and Israel, my heritage." The new fusion of individual and society, society and nature, body and spirit, and social duty with ecstatic celebration, Waskow sees as the genius of the Jewish tradition which coincides with the vision of human liberation today. The Jewish community, both in Israel and in the Diaspora, must be both for its own liberation and that of all men in a prophetic tension between its actuality and its redemptive promise. This demands a religious and not merely a secular or national identity of the Jew.

Has Waskow's vision solved on a new level that insoluble dilemma of the dispersed Jew which Memmi believed could not be solved within the context created by the hostile self-definition of the gentile community toward the Jews? Such a new option is still in jeopardy if one assumes, as Memmi does, that gentile attitudes toward Jews are unalterably fixed by the totalistic universalism of a Christian fulfilled messianism. Such a Christian theological stance demands, in some form, the drawing of a mental ghetto of negation around those who reject this fundamental Christian self-affirmation. But should Christians really believe in their messianism in this form, or hasn't this very history demonstrated its false ideological character? This demands nothing less than a fundamental rethinking of the meaning of the basic proposition of Christian faith that "Jesus is the Christ." A Christian assertion that Jesus is the "Messiah of Israel," which contradicts the fundamental meaning of what Israel means by "Messiah," is and always has been fundamentally questionable. That questionableness must now be clarified and unambiguously applied to the historic sin of its translation into the negation of the Jews. This demands a relativizing of the identification of Jesus as the Christ. Contextually we can speak of Jesus as the "messianic experience for us," but that way of speaking doesn't make this experience self-enclosed, but points beyond itself to a liberation still to come. Both the original roots of Christian faith and the dilemma of modern Christology will make it evident that such an affirmation of the messianic event in Jesus in a contextual and open-ended, rather than a "once for all" and absolutistic way, is demanded by the exigencies of Christian theology itself. In this way the Christian experience can parallel rather than negate the liberation experiences which are the community symbols of other faiths. For the Jews, the Exodus experience is also a very real actuality of liberation which is, at the same time, a hope for a liberation still to come. In this way the Jew and the Christian stand in parallel traditions, each having tasted grace, each looking for a fulfillment that is "beyond." Instead of an absolutized revelation which must negate and displace that of Judaism, both communities see themselves as walking in the same human condition, between slavery and the Promised Land, amid many a golden idol and broken tablet. Only by a fundamental critique of its falsely ideological way of defining the messianic experience in Jesus can Christianity cease to draw a special circle of rejection around the Jews and bring to an end that *galut* defined by Christian theological identity *vis à vis* the Jews. Then for the first time, Christianity and Judaism as brother peoples, can work on that common *galut* of human alienation which separates us all from the Promised Land of freedom, justice and peace.

Chapter 7

Is Christianity Misogynist?
The Failure of Women's
Liberation in the Church

The oppression of women is undoubtedly the oldest form of oppression in human history. From the dawn of history the physical lightness of the woman's body (which has nothing to do with biological inferiority) and the fact that the woman is the childbearer have been used to subordinate the woman to the man in a chattel status and to deprive women of the leadership possibilities and the cultural development of the dominant group. The oppression of women can be seen as falling into two distinct cultural stages, corresponding to tribal societies and classical civilizations, while the liberation of women awaits the flowering of that modern civilization which has overcome the dichotomized reality principle of classical cultures. Religions have played a key role in both stages, since it was religion that formulated the world view and prescribed the rituals which inculcated that world view at each stage of consciousness.

The tribal period is one which must be studied much more carefully relative to the oppression of women. There was a time when the tribal period was seen as a time of female dominance, of "matriarchy," while the oppression of women came in only with private property and the division of labor in classical civilizations. Marxist theory preserved a version of this nineteenth century anthropology. The tribal period thus became a kind of "golden age" that served as a point of reference for the future liberation. It now appears clear that "matriarchy" was a method of reckoning descent through the mother, but this never entailed women as the power-holders in society. Agricultural societies clearly developed a different symbolism than hunting and nomadic societies. Women were innovators in the technology of agriculture at an early period and the connection of women and the earth as the sources of fecundity gave feminine symbols and feminine goddesses a primacy in agricultural religions.

In pastoral and hunting societies the disability of the woman, especially when pregnant, was more evident. In these societies strict segregation of women from the male hunting lodge, where the tribesmen prepared themselves for hunting and war, was developed. H. A. Hays, in his comprehensive volume on the history of the oppression of women, *The Dangerous Sex; The Myth of Feminine Evil* details the exorbitant disabilities heaped on women in these tribal societies. Normative sexuality was defined from the perspective of male sexuality. From this perspective the woman was seen as a deviant, an aberration. The vagina was seen as a wound, and the fact that a woman bled from the vagina a mark of castration. Terrible fears and taboos built up around this strange interpretation of woman's sexuality as a wound and a castration which might, through some evil influence, be visited upon the male penis. (It is interesting to see that Freud, whose views were taken to be "scientific," reproduces a psychological doctrine based essentially on this ancient misconception.) The aberrant or castrated sexuality of women was interpreted as "bad mana" from which men must rigidly protect themselves. Menstruation, childbirth, everything connected with the sexuality of women, and finally, even the very presence of women, came to be seen as "unclean"; a debilitating influence that might threaten the virility of the male. Women were isolated from each other and hedged in with elaborate purification rituals which often forced them to live by themselves in places of harsh segregation during large parts of their lives. Social relations were severely restricted, so that women, while preparing the food for the family, often were not allowed to sit at table with the men, but must hide in the back of the house lest their presence during the consumption of the strength-giving food cast an evil spell on male power.

By contrast, the male lodge became the place of male bonding and reinforcement in power. The relations of the males in the male lodge were at once both hierarchical and sado-masochistic, and these painful homosexual rituals were an intrinsic part of that male bonding that fit the tribesmen, as a caste, for hunting and war. Mysterious noises from the bull-roarer and other instruments emitted from the male lodge, reinforcing the males in their sense of collective power, while frightening the women who were strictly excluded from knowing anything of what was taking place inside. Hays sees this male lodge and its rituals as the precursor of all those exclusively male fraternities, from armies to monasteries to press clubs, where men reinforce themselves in their power against women, and practice a strict pecking order among themselves.

The practices described by Hays as characteristic of hunting tribes would seem to have little connection with higher religions, yet, in fact, these practices were carried over into the great basins of civilization when hunting and nomadic peoples invaded and settled these regions. Israel was just such a tribe, and it canonized the ancient taboos and rituals of uncleanness against women in the Torah and the Talmud and thus passed down this set of attitudes and practices to the present day. This view of women as ritually unclean was transmitted to Christianity, in turn, and shapes to a remarkable extent the laws about women in classical Christian canon law. As Clara Maria Henning, one of the few Roman Catholic canon lawyers in the world, says in her article on the attitude toward women in Catholic canon law,[1] the basic concept of women in canon law is the ancient concept of uncleanness, extended into the Christian ascetic idea of woman as a sexual threat. Most of the laws having to do with women revolve around elaborate exclusions from contact with priests and contact with the sacred ceremonies where priests preside. These laws command women to cover their heads, forbid them to approach the altar during the celebration or to enter the sanctuary during Mass; exclude them from acting as servers at Mass, and even discourage them from singing and other participation. Not surprisingly, in the light of what we have said about the origins of these attitudes in ancient tribal taboos, the most vehement laws against women revolve around their sexual uncleanness during menstruation and childbearing. This view of women as unclean was crucial in the final demise of the institution of deaconesses in the early Church. It surrounded women with a ritual of purification after childbirth, and forbade her, at certain points in the Church's history, from taking communion or even entering the church during menstruation.

It might have been thought that the rise of the classical civilizations might have overcome these disabilities heaped upon women in hunting societies, since now mental quickness, rather than physical prowess, became the more important power. Woman's wit is clearly equal to that of the man. Therefore the transformation from physical to mental power should have given women the opportunity to overcome these ancient taboos. However, instead, the prejudice against women was translated into the intellectual sphere, and men reconfirmed their right to be the stronger by declaring that they alone possessed genuine mental power and all the spiritual virtues that went with it, while women were identified with the body and what was seen as the "lower psyche." Thus the actual capacity of women to intellectual equality and to parity within a civilization based on cultural rather than physical prowess was elaborately suppressed in classical civilizations by a cultural denial to women of these capacities and the institutionalization of this denial through the exclusion of women from opportunities for education and formation in higher culture. This exclusion of women from education lasted down into the late nineteenth century, when women fought a long battle to be admitted first to secondary and then to higher education, encountering male opposition at every step of the way. Not too surprisingly, the argument that was constantly used against the right of women to education was the insistence that woman lacked such capacity by nature, and that she was peculiarly tied up, psychosomatically, with childbearing, so that any diversion of her "blood" to her brain would divert it from the one place that it was necessary, namely her womb, and render her infertile! Clergymen were the warmest advocates of this particular piece of misinformation.[2]

Classical civilizations created a dualistic view of soul and body as an expression of their struggle to assert the ascendancy of the intellectual principle over the givenness of the human condition. But they also repressed the possibility for the liberation of women that arose out of that development, by equating soul-body dualism with male-female dualism, and thus reestablishing the subordination of women in new form. Christianity, in this respect, was the heir and bearer of the culture of classical civilization. And the study of the attitude toward women in the Church Fathers reveals dramatically both sides of this new development; the potential for the liberation of women through the affirmation of the superiority of the spiritual to the somatic principle, and the suppression of this possibility by equating the feminine with the bodily principle.

The dualistic anthropology, which Christianity absorbed from Platonism, created a distinct tension between its ascetic spirituality and the body-affirming doctrine of creation which was found in the Hebrew Scriptures. Eastern Christian theology tried to solve this conflict by defining the original creation as spiritual and monistic and ascribing the "gross" body and bi-sexuality to the fall.[3] Latin theology, in St. Augustine, for example, attempted to affirm the bi-sexual, bodily character of the original creation, but in a way that equated soul-body dualism with male-female dualism. Thus the spiritual image of God (made in the image of the divine *Logos*—Christ) in man became essentially male, and femaleness was equated with the lower, corporeal nature.

For Augustine, the original Adam was unitary in person, but compound in nature, consisting of male spirit and female bodiliness. When Eve was taken from the side of Adam, she stood for the bodily "side" of man which was taken from him in order to serve him as a helpmate. But she is a helpmate solely for the task of procreation, in which she is alone indispensable. For any spiritual task, another male would be more suitable.[4] So the purpose of woman's existence was defined essentially in terms of childbearing. Other than this there is no reason for the existence of woman. Inexplicably, Augustine also affirms that Eve too has a rational spirit, being also a compound of body and spirit. But Augustine persists in speaking of woman, in relation to the male, as standing for the relation of body to spirit. Moreover, he consistently defines this relationship as woman's "nature." [5] He thus concludes that the male alone possesses the full image of God, whereas woman, when taken by herself, does not possess the full image of God, but only when taken together with the male who "is her head." [6] Woman is therefore defined as a *relative being*, who exists only in relationship to the male, who alone possesses full autonomous personhood. This view of woman is perhaps the ultimate core of misogynism.

This assimilation of male-female dualism into soul-body dualism conditions the definition of woman both in terms of the order of nature and in terms of the condition of the fall. In the order of nature woman is essentially subordinate to the man, just as the body is essentially subordinate to the mind in that right ordering of body to spirit that is defined as "original justice." (!) But because ascetic spirituality defined sin as the disordering of the flesh to the spirit, which made the mind the subject of passions, the equation of woman with body also made her peculiarly the symbol of sin. This double definition of woman, as submissive body in the order of nature, and "carnality" in the disorder of sin, allows the Church Fathers to slip somewhat inconsistently from the second to the first, and attribute an inferiority in women that is sinful to woman's "nature." In some of the Church Fathers, such as Tertullian, the sinfulness of woman is equated with her primary responsibility for the original fall of man. Tertullian speaks of woman's role in the fall by such epithets as "the Devil's gateway," and sees her nature as permanently marked by her special guilt in causing the fall of man, leading up to the necessity for the death of Christ.[7]

St. Augustine is somewhat more temperate in his diatribes against Eve as the cause of the fall. Augustine's stress falls much more on the natural inferiority of women, as body, in the relation of body to mind in the right ordering of nature. For him, the fall could occur only when the mind consents to "go along," and not simply when the body "tempts." But this does not imply a milder view of sin, but rather a more contemptuous view of woman's ability to cause the fall "by herself." [8]

This assimilation of femaleness into bodiliness allows Augustine to explain woman's subjugation in the order of nature, but it makes for some contradiction when it comes to defending woman's redeemability; her capacity, like the male, to overcome the body and rise to the higher, spiritual nature (the Patristic definition of redemption). Augustine attempts to explain this contradiction by distinguishing what woman *is,* where she is equivalent to the male, and what she *symbolizes* in her bodily nature, where she stands for the subjugation of body to spirit in nature and that debasing carnality which draws the male mind down from its heavenly heights to "wallow in the flesh." As he puts it in his *Soliloquies:*

I feel that nothing so casts down the manly mind from its heights as the fondling of woman and those bodily contacts which belong to the married state.[9]

But since Augustine identifies this that woman "symbolizes," with her "nature," this creates a strange schizophrenia in the relation of the male to the female in marriage. The man is exhorted to love his wife's spiritual nature, but to despise in her all her bodily functions as woman and wife:

A good Christian is found, toward one and the same woman, to love the creature of God whom he desires to be transformed and renewed, but to hate in her the corruptible and mortal conjugal connection, sexual intercourse and all that pertains to her as a wife.[10]

It never occurs to Augustine that this definition of woman's nature in terms of what she "symbolizes" in the eye of the male perception, rather than in terms of what she is in herself, might be precisely a disorder in the eye of the male perceiver, and therefore in no sense a stance for the definition of woman's nature! But, for Augustine, as for the tradition of male dominance generally, this androcentric perspective, which reduced woman to "body" vis à vis the male eye, is never questioned, but is presumed. The essence of male ideology can be said to be contained precisely in this cultural relationship, where the woman is the one acted upon and defined by the male perception and "use," and her own self-definition and perspective are never heard or incorporated culturally. Women, as all oppressed people, live in a culture of silence, as objects, never subjects of the relationship.

The definition of woman as body lends itself to an identification of the female psyche and personality as peculiarly characterized by "carnal" traits. To woman's "mind" are attributed essentially the traits of pettiness, sensuality, materialism and maliciousness, while all the virtues of the mind, such as chastity, patience, wisdom, temperance, fortitude and justice, are equated with masculinity.[11] This comes about with a kind of spiritualizing of the primitive equation of all that is "strong" with the male; all that is weak with the female.

This definition of woman, both physically and psychically, in terms of the lower nature, creates a peculiar contradiction when it comes time to defend the ability of the "virgin" to overcome this lower nature and be redeemed. It becomes characteristic of the Fathers, the ascetic writers especially, to speak of the virgin as having become "male," by transcending the female nature, physically and psychically. The very possibility of redemption through spiritualization is thus, for woman, "unnatural"; a transcendence of her "nature"; whereas the male ascetic is seen as being restored to his natural male spirituality through redemption. This view extended itself into a debate over the sexual character of the risen body. It was natural to conclude, therefore, that in the resurrection from the dead, there would be only males, females being transformed into males.

(This is analogous to the racist view in Mormonism that only whites are redeemable, so the Negro can be saved only by being transformed into a white person.) Augustine and Jerome both assert that mankind will arise in both male and female bodies, but they too find the incompatibility so strong that they must modify this view by asserting that these bodies will be spiritual and lacking in all sensual libido, the female risen body in particular having been deprived of those organs having to do with intercourse and childbearing, so that the female body becomes "suited to glory rather than to shame."

What this angelic hysterectomy is supposed to mean is anyone's guess, but it illustrates graphically the dilemma of Patristic anthropology. They wish to affirm a doctrine of redemption that coheres with the original bodily, bi-sexual nature which God had declared "very good" in the beginning; but since they have declared this to be "very bad" and define redemption as the overcoming of the body, sexual relationship and female nature, they can only affirm this continuity by peculiarly mutilating redemption or creation or both in these particular characteristics.

The Fathers never entirely deny, although they often seem to forget, that woman too has a spiritual nature equivalent to that of the male. Indeed this affirmation is assumed in that view which allows the woman, as well as the man, to become a "virgin" and to rise to the "higher life" of monistic spirituality. But since woman is also made, in her bodily nature, peculiarly the symbol of body in relation to the (male) mind and associated with all the sensual and depraved characteristics of psychology through this corporeality, her salvation then is seen, not as an affirmation of her (feminine) nature, but a transcendence of her (feminine) nature to a higher (male) possibility. Such a view forces upon the female ascetic both a redoubled subjugation of her body and personality in ascetic practices, and also an abasement of her "image," so that she will no longer appear as an attractive female body before the male visual perception. This obsession with blotting out the female bodily image explains that peculiar concern in Patristic literature with matters of female dress, adornment and physical appearance which still agitates the relationship of the Vatican congregation for religious in its relation to its daughters! The woman must be stripped of all adornment that reveals or enhances her femininity. She must bear an unshapely dress and veil that conceal her face and limbs. Finally, she must literally destroy her physical appearance with dirt and fasting, so that she becomes unsightly. As Tertullian puts it, in his treatise, *de cultu feminarum:*

> It is time for you to know that not merely must the pageantry of ficticious and elaborate beauty be rejected by you, but even that natural grace must be obliterated by concealment and negligence, as equally dangerous to the glances of the beholder's eye.[12]

The definition of sin as sexual and bodily feeling, of course, creates that rigid view of the right purpose and use of sex characteristic of Augustine, that has traditionally denied the possibility of birth control. Since women are the childbearers, this means, in effect, the denial of the right of women to limit or control the effects of male sexual use of their bodies. When the denial of birth control is taken together with the view (also accepted by the Fathers), that woman stands in a chattel relation to the male in marriage, i.e., the husband has a proprietary right over his wife's body, which forbids the wife to deny her husband sexual access to her at any time, the subordination of woman to biological necessity becomes complete.

Augustine believed that, in the original creation, there would have been bi-sexual, but non-sensual, reproduction. In paradise woman would have been perfectly submissive to the male, just as the body would have been perfectly submissive to the mind. Just as every organ and muscle in the body would have been completely under the control and command of the mind; i.e., man would have been able to whistle tunes with his anus (!), so the female (body) would also have been perfectly submissive to the mind of the directing male. Man would have used the female body for reproduction, but in a completely dispassionate way, just as the farmer sows his seed in the furrow of a field. This act would have been entirely purposive; i.e., done solely for procreation, and would have been devoid of all sensual feelings.[13] Man's sexual organ would have been totally under the control of his rational mind, so that he would have moved it to its purpose just as he moves his hand or his foot now, without any rush of sensual feeling accompanying this act. Thus, in Augustine's view, rightly ordered sex is such as to be depersonalized, unfeeling and solely instrumental. It relates to the woman literally as a "baby making machine"; i.e., a body whose sole purpose for existence is to be used as the incubator of the male seed.

When, however, man sins, he loses the "original justice" of this ordering of body to mind. Sinful "carnality," signifying the revolt of the sensual principle against its "head," enters in. Then the male loses control over his sexual organ, which begins to respond with a "will of its own" to the female bodily presence. This Augustine sees as the exemplification of the principle of sin, whereby the "law of the members wars against the law of the mind." [14] For Augustine, then, the spontaneous tumescence of the male penis, in response to sensual stimuli, and independent of conscious control, is the very essence of sin. He proceeded to construct his whole doctrine of the transmission of sin around this view.

Ideally, the married couple should give themselves to the sexual act solely for the purpose of procreation. Otherwise they should be continent. However, since the fall, this dispassionate and wholly instrumental use of sex, such as would have existed in paradise is no longer possible. The sexual organs have been disordered by sin and so cause an unruly by-product of sensual pleasure, whether the couple will or not. Augustine sees this spontaneous libido as intrinsically sinful. It is forgiven to the married couple only if it is not intended, if it is despised by them, and their intention remains solely that of procreation. But the sinful character of the means, nevertheless, conditions the end product in the child, who is born thereby tainted with Original Sin.[15] This then is the means whereby the original sin of Adam, with its disordering of the relation of flesh to spirit, is transmitted from generation to generation through the sexual act.

If the couple actually intend to enjoy carnal pleasure, although also intending and not impeding procreation, Augustine sees this as sinful, but venially so, since it is allowable under that apostolic concession that it is better to "marry than to burn." It was this second purpose of the sexual act that was spoken of as the "remedy for concupiscence." But it is allowable only as a concession to weakness and is not a good in itself.[16] Finally, if the couple desires "only" carnal pleasure and impedes procreation (and this would include the rhythm method, for Augustine, which was practiced by the Manichaeans), the act is wholly sinful and equivalent to fornication.[17] Such a narrow view of sex follows from a depersonalized definition of the sexual relationship, which is seen either as instrumental or narcissistically carnal. The possibility of bodily relation as an interpersonal relationship or a vehicle of love, is essentially eliminated. Augustine does speak of a third purpose of marriage as a "symbol" of unity, mirroring the relationship of Christ to the Church, but he never develops this as an inter-personality that could be expressed through the sexual act itself. Indeed this third purpose remains wholly undefined in his thought, and he speaks of the possibility of friendship between the married as arising only when the sexual act is no longer used, as in old people.[18]

This depersonalization of the sexual act and through it the depersonalization of woman must be seen as the reflection of that fundamental assimilation of male-female relation into soul-body relation. This implies a subject-object relationship between men and women. For the soul-body relationship corresponds to the subject-object relationship between the subject and that external reality which is reduced to the status of a "thing" to be "used." This subject-object relationship has, as its basic characteristic, the negating of the other as a "thou" or equivalent "subject," and therefore abolishes the possibility of a relation to the "other" as one of mutuality and intersubjectivity. The translation of male-female dualism in Christianity into soul-body dualism, therefore, blotted out in classical spirituality, the possibility of bodily relationship as a meeting of persons. It constricted it into the framework of a relation of a subject to an object to be "used." Woman, then, was defined literally as a "sex object," either to be rightly used, for procreation, or wrongly used, narcissistically, for carnal pleasure. In either case, woman as a person never appears in the relationship.

This view of sexuality determines the three basic images of women in the Church Fathers; woman as whore; woman as wife and woman as virgin. As whore, woman represents sinful carnality which is the essence of the fall. Here, woman is depicted as the bold strumpet, strutting forth in all her natural and artificial bodily allures. Here, woman incarnates the very character of the sensual principle in revolt against its "head," that subverts the right ordering between mind and sense.

As wife, woman is also defined as body, but now as submissive body, obedient to her "head," that stands for the proper relationship of the sensual to the intellectual principle. The ideal for the wife was one of total servility and meekness, even under harsh and unjust treatment. The wife is seen as having no personal rights autonomously, either over her mind or over her body. Mentally she is said to have "no head," but to submit to her husband who "is her head," while, on the bodily level the husband has complete proprietary rights to her body and the property of the household.[19] This rigid view of the mental and psychical subjugation of the wife is illustrated in a letter which Augustine wrote to the North African matron Ecducia.[20] This woman apparently had chosen a life of continence that had become contrary to her husband's wishes, although he had originally agreed to it. Augustine allows her to continue only because the husband had once agreed, but he severely rebukes her for her disposal of family property without her husband's permission. He enunciates the basic principles which guide his view, in the process. Women may never, independently, choose continence, or deny sexual use of their bodies to their husbands, because the woman has "no head of her own," but belongs to her husband, who "is her head," and it is a sin for the woman to refuse to her husband the "debt" of her body.

For Augustine, the ideal wife should receive no sensual pleasure from such sexual use, but submit her body solely as

an instrument for procreation. Augustine even rationalizes Old
Testament polygamy on these grounds, arguing that these ancient worthies gave themselves such excessive "marrying and
giving in marriage," without experiencing any sensual pleasure,
but solely in obedience to God's command to (hurry up and)
increase and multiply, so they might all the sooner make up
the whole of the race of Israel from which the messiah was
to be born. Polygamy was admissible for this purpose, although polyandry would have been unacceptable, since, as
Augustine puts it, "nature allows multiplicity in subjugations,
but demands singularity in dominations," just as many members
may serve the one head in the body, and many slaves the one
master, but not vice versa.[21] Here we can see how fundamental
it was for Augustine to equate male-female dualism with soul-
body dualism in a way that defines that relationship essentially
as one of domination and subjugation. The husband was, of
course, exhorted to love his wife and not abuse her, but again
this is said to be as he would "love his own body," and because
it would demean his dignity as the "head" to do otherwise.[22]
It is not because women have any autonomous dignity as persons, or rights over their own bodies relative to the male. Such
a theory of married women in Christianity not only did not lift
up the social position of women beyond what it had been in
antiquity, but even fell below those modest legal rights to personal and economic autonomy which women had been win-
ning under later Roman law. Thus the frequent claim that
Christianity elevated the position of woman must be denied. It
actually lowered the position of woman relative to the more
enlightened legislation of later Roman society, and elevated
woman only in her new role as "virgin."

For the Fathers, marriage has the lowest place of honor in
the scheme of Christian life. Now that Christ has come, marriage
is still allowable, but no longer necessary, since marrying and
giving in marriage has been superceded by the new order of the
Resurrection. The blessings upon procreation from the Old
Testament, therefore, have been rescinded. Procreation is not
forbidden, to be sure, but it has become redundant and dis-

tracting. It would be better if all men imitated the way of Christian perfection and refrained from procreation, so that the world could come to an end the faster, and the new world of the Resurrection could dawn in its entirety, according to Augustine.[23] If a Christian is truly converted, he will become continent. The married life thus falls at the bottom of the hierarchy of virtue, falls below that 100-fold virtue of virginity, or the 60-fold virtue of widowhood.[24] The life of continence is the only life fully compatible with the Christian life of spiritual regeneration.

The highest ideal of life, then, for the woman is virginity. Here alone does woman rise to spirituality, personhood and equality with the male. But only at the expense of crushing out of her being all vestiges of her bodily and her female "natures" and rising to "unnatural manliness." But this regeneration is not seen as releasing the woman for a boldness and autonomy, since the condition for this release of her spiritual principle is that total abasement of her body and her female image which, *de facto,* lies under obedience to male authority. This assertion that female virginity in no way undid the hierarchical relation of male to female in the Church clearly ran into some real contradiction during the first period of the Christian ascetic movement. The Church Fathers, unwittingly, in their ascetic doctrines, released a movement of women's liberation which suggested a far fuller equality of male and female under the new order of the Resurrection. Again and again the early ascetic writers enunciated the principle that Eve was punished for her sin by the twofold marks of bearing children in sorrow and being under the authority of the husband. In choosing the life of virginity, the woman was declared to have thrown off both of these marks of Eve's punishment.[25] While it was fairly easy to see how the virgin no longer bore children in sorrow (since she bore no children at all), the implication of virginity as releasing women from male subjugation was clearly one that the Church Fathers were quite unwilling to push to its logical conclusions. But there was a powerful movement of feminine asceticism in the fourth century and thereafter which clearly read this doctrine quite differently, and did indeed assume that the choice of the life of continence released them from male authority in general, and not merely in the literal sense that they had no husbands to whom to be subjugated. Thus many women flocked to the life of continence, either by refusing to marry or else by separating from their husbands to form communities of women, and were claiming thereby a freedom and equality with men. One peculiar expression of this was the "spiritual marriage" in which the virgin lived in a spiritual relationship with a male ascetic. In some cases this probably worked to the disadvantage of women, who were forced into a kind of housekeeper relationship. But clearly, in the case of a strong-minded female ascetic, it could constitute something like a free love relationship, as is evident from some of Jerome's horrified descriptions of this possibility.[26] The idea that the woman who chose continence freed herself from the twofold curse of Eve of childbearing and male domination was leading many women in this period to abandon their children and household responsibilities, and depart to found communities of women. It was only with the greatest difficulty that the Church brought this female ascetic movement under control, but arguing simultaneously that, while virginity did raise the woman above her "female nature" to a virility and spiritual equality with the male, this in no way detracted from male authority, because the condition for this spiritualization was her self-abasement, humility and obedience to God (*de facto* exercised by male authority in the Church). The insistence that the male alone could represent Christ in the priesthood (since he alone possesses that spiritual image of God that mirrors the divine Word), and the continuation of the Jewish ideas of woman's uncleanliness, operated to exclude women from any positions of authority in the Church and thus to insure that, however high a woman might rise in the female ascetic ranks, there would always be a male authority above her. Needless to say this tension between the female ascetic movement and male authority is exploding all over again in contemporary Catholicism, having been successfully repressed for fourteen hundred years!

Thus the potential of the female ascetic movement to express the liberation of women within the framework of classical religion was largely repressed in Christianity through the very dualism in which the liberation of the spiritual principle from the body was perceived. At each point the women found femininity equated with bodiliness to re-subordinate her, even as an ascetic, to the right of the stronger, now interpreted spiritually as the right of the male to monopolize intellectual power and identify it with masculinity.

Nevertheless the ascetic movement in late antiquity did raise up a new cultural ideal of the "spiritual woman," who, through the conquest of the body, could rise to spiritual personhood equal to that of the male and could even achieve the life of intellectual contemplation that led to the ultimate *summum bonum* of communion with God. Women now, for the first time, were conceded the possibility of the highest spiritual achievement, from which they were generally excluded among Greek philosophers (although late antiquity did see one great woman philosopher, Hypatia). Judaism, by contrast, systematically excluded women from living the life of the scholar. In Christianity women, normally, and in great numbers, were admitted to the highest ideals of ascetic spirituality. Fourth and fifth century Christianity, moreover, saw a great flowering of cultural imagery related to spiritual femininity. Much of the literature of the period was constructed around the figure of the woman as seer, muse or revealer of spiritual truths, from the figure of "Dame Church," who speaks to the worried Christian in the *Shepherd of Hermas* in the second century, to "Dame Philosophia" who is Boethius' muse in prison four centuries later. As the Virgin Psyche, the feminine principle in the soul was represented as the human partner in the nuptial mystery of the communion of the soul with Christ in mystical ecstacy. As the Bridal Church, woman represents mankind in its eschatological union with God. All these images of spiritual womanhood were gathered together to make up that Mariology which flowered, together with the ascetic movement, in the fourth and fifth centuries. The culmination of this elevation of spiritual femininity was the doctrine of Mary's Assumption, a characteristic doctrine of this period of the Church's history. The doctrine of the Assumption grew up first in Egypt in the early fourth century, in the cradle of Christian asceticism, and spread from there essentially along with the spread of the ascetical movement. In the doctrine of the Assumption, the "Spiritual Woman" was raised to the very heavens, to take her place beside the Jewish Ancient of Days and his Son Messiah who once had ruled from the Cherubim Throne in exclusive patriarchal splendor. An early precedent for this, however, was set within Judaism itself which used the femininity of the word "spirit" in Hebrew to speak of God's Spirit as the "Eldest daughter of Yahweh," "who sits at his right hand." Christianity inherited this tradition in the form of Sophia piety that also merged with Mariology in the Eastern Church.

But in ascetical Christianity this elevation of spiritual womanhood was done at the price of despising all real, living women, sex and fecundity, and the sublimation of the feminine into an ethereal love object for the sublimated sexual libido of the male ascetic. It should not surprise us, therefore, that Mariology has done little for the liberation of women, concretely and historically, when we realize to what extent it was created by and has always been the spirituality of male ascetics, serving as a substitute fantasized love object for a repressed male sexual libido, thereby guarding this from turning back to any real, physical expression of love with the dangerous daughters of Eve! Yet perhaps the task of Christians today is not merely to vilify the inhumanity of this tradition both to the affections of men and the natural somatic persons and full development of women. Rather we must realize how this ideology fits in with a strange but real struggle of mankind for transcendence of their given situation and the achievements of spiritual personhood, which seems to lie behind this aberrant fear of the body and its feelings. Without discarding these achievements, we today must find out how to pour them back into a full-bodied sense of creation and incarnation, as male and female, who can begin to stand as personalized, autonomous selves and therefore as full persons for each other, not merely against the body, but in and through the body.[27]

NOTES

1. See the article by Clara Maria Henning, "Canon Law and the Battle of the Sexes," in the *Images of Women in the Judaeo-Christian tradition,* edited by Rosemary Ruether (Simon and Schuster, 1973).

2. See Rosemary Ruether, "Are Women's Colleges Obsolete," *Critic,* Oct.-Nov., (1968), pp. 58-64, for a summary of this struggle for women's education in America.

3. Origen's, *de Principiis* and Gregory Nyssa's *de opificio hominis.*

4. Augustine, *de grat. Ch. et pecc. orig.* 2,40; *de Genesi ad Lit.* 9,5.

5. Augustine's *Confessiones* 13,32; *de opere Monach.* 40.

6. Augustine, *de Trinitate* 7,7,10.

7. Tertullian, *de cultu fem.* 1,1.

8. Augustine, *de contin.* 1,23; *civitate Dei* 14,11; *de Genesi ad Lit.* 11,42.

9. Augustine, *Soliloquies* 1,10.

10. Augustine, *de sermone Dom. in Monte* 41.

11. *Eg.* Leander of Seville, *de instit. Virg;* Ambrose, *de Cain et Abel* 1,4; Jerome, *Ep.* 130,17.

12. Tertullian, *de cultu fem.* 2,2.

13. Augustine, *civitate Dei* 14,26; *contra Julian* 3,13,27; *de grat. Ch. et pecc orig.* 2,40.

14. Romans 8,23; Augustine, *civitate Dei* 14,24; *de grat. Ch. et pecc. orig.* 2,41; *de nupt. et concup.* 1,6-7,27,33.

15. Augustine, *de pecc. merit. et remiss.* 1,29; *de grat. Ch. et pecc. orig.* 1,27; 2,41-44; *de nupt. et concup.* 1,13,22; *adv. Julian,* 3,7; 5,14.

16. Jerome, *Ep.* 48,14; Augustine, *de nupt, et concup,* 1,16; *de bono conj.* 6,11.

17. Augustine, *de nupt et concup,* 1,17; *de bono conj.* 10,11; *de conj. adult.* 2,12.

18. Augustine, *de grat. Ch. et pecc. orig,* 2,39; *de nupt, et concup.* 1,19; *de bono conj.* 17; *de Genesi ad lit.* 9,7.

19. *Eg.* John Chrysostom, *Epist. ad Ephes.; hom.* 13; *hom.* 22; and *hom.* 26,8.

20. Augustine, *Ep.* 262, to Ecducia.

21. Augustine, *de bono conj.* 17-20; *de nupt. et concup.* 1,9-10.

22. John Chrysostom, *Epis. ad Ephes.; hom.* 26,8; also Augustine, *de conj. adult.* 2,15.

23. Compare Jerome, *adv. Jov,* 1,36; Augustine, *de nupt. et concup.* 1,14-15; *de bono conj.* 10,13; *de bono viduit,* 8-11; *de sancta virg.* 9,9,16.

24. This common image contrasting marriage, widowhood and virginity according to the 30, 60 and 100 fold harvest of Mark 4,20 is found repeatedly in the Fathers; *eg.* Cyprian, *de habitu virg.* 21; Athanasius, *Ep.* 48,2; Tertullian, *de exhort, cast.* 1; Jerome, *Epp.* 22,15; 48,3; 66,2; 120, 1,9; *Adv. Jov.* 1,3; Augustine, *de sancta virg.* 45; Ambrose, *de virg.* 1,60.

25. Cyprian, *de habitu virg.* 22; Jerome, *Ep.* 130,8; *Comm. in Epist. ad Ephes.* 3,5; *adv. Helvid.* 22; Leander of Seville, *de instit. virg.*

26. Jerome, *Ep.* 117.

27. A fuller exposition of the material of this chapter is found in my chapter on "Misogynism and Virginal Feminism in the Fathers of the Church," in the book edited by this author, *Images of Women in the Judaeo-Christian Tradition* (Simon and Schuster, 1973).

Chapter 8

Mother Earth and the Megamachine: A Theology of Liberation in a Feminine, Somatic and Ecological Perspective

Christianity, as the heir of both classical Neo-Platonism and apocalyptic Judaism, combines the image of a male, warrior God with the exaltation of the intellect over the body. The Classical doctrine of Christ, which fused the vision of the heavenly messianic king with the transcendent *logos* of immutable Being, was a synthesis of the religious impulses of late antique religious consciousness, but precisely in their alienated state of development. These world-negating religions carried a set of dualities that still profoundly condition the modern world view.

All the basic dualities—the alienation of the mind from the body; the alienation of the subjective self from the objective world; the subjective retreat of the individual, alienated from the social community; the domination or rejection of nature by spirit—these all have roots in the apocalyptic-Platonic religious heritage of classical Christianity. But the alienation of the masculine from the feminine is the primary sexual symbolism that sums up all these alienations. The psychic traits of intellectuality, transcendent spirit and autonomous will that were identified with the male left the woman with the contrary traits of bodiliness, sensuality and subjugation. Society, through the centuries, has in every way profoundly conditioned men and women to play out their lives and find their capacities within this basic antithesis.

This antithesis has also shaped the modern technological environment. The plan of our cities is made in this image: the sphere of domesticity, rest and child-rearing where women are segregated is clearly separated from those corridors down which men advance in assault upon the world of "work." The woman who tries to break out of the female sphere into the masculine finds not only psychic conditioning and social attitudes but the structure of social reality itself ranged against her.

The physical environment—access to basic institutions in terms of space and time—has been shaped for the fundamental purpose of freeing one half of the race for the work society calls "productive," while the other half of the race remains in a sphere that services this freedom for work. The woman who would try to occupy both spheres at once literally finds *reality itself* stacked against her, making the combination of maternal and masculine occupations all but impossible without extraordinary energy or enough wealth to hire domestic help.

Thus, in order to play out the roles shaped by this definition of the male life style, the woman finds that she must either be childless or have someone else act as her "wife" (i.e., play the service role for her freedom to work). Women's liberation is therefore *impossible* within the present social system except for an elite few. Women simply cannot be persons within the present system of work and family, and they can only rise to liberated personhood by the most radical and fundamental reshaping of the entire human environment in a way that redefines the very nature of work, family and the institutional expressions of social relations.

Although widespread hopes for liberty and equality among all humans rose with the *philosophes* of the Enlightenment, hardly any of these ideologies of the French Revolution and the liberal revolutions of the nineteenth century envisioned the liberation of women. The bourgeoisie, the workers, the peasants, even the Negro slaves were more obvious candidates for liberation, while the subjugation of women continued to be viewed as an unalterable necessity of nature. When the most radical of the French liberals, the Marquis de Condorcet, included women in the vision of equality, his colleagues thought he had lost his senses and breached the foundations of the new rationalism. The ascendency of Reason meant the ascendency of the intellect over the passions, and this must ever imply the subjugation of women.

An embarrassed silence or cries of ridicule likewise greeted this topic when it was raised half a century later by another consistent libertarian, John Stuart Mill. Only after a long struggle from the nineteenth to the early twentieth century did women finally break down the barriers that separated them from the most basic rights to work, education, financial autonomy and full citizenship—and even these freedoms are not universally secured today.

The reaction against and suppression of the Woman's Liberation Movement has been closely tied to reactionary cultural and political movements, and the emancipated woman has been the chief target of elitism, fascism and neoconservatism of all kinds. The Romantic Movement traumatized Europe's reaction to the French Revolution, reinstated the traditional view of women in idealized form, while the more virulent blood-and-soil reactionaries of the nineteenth century expressed a more naked misogynism. Literary figures such as Strindberg and Nietzsche couldn't stress strongly enough their abhorrence of women. At the turn of the century. Freud codified all the traditional negative views of the female psychology, giving them scientific respectability for the new psychological and social sciences. These negative stereotypes have been a key element in the repression of the women's movement through the popular mass media.

In Nazism the reactionary drive against the libertarian tradition culminated in a virulent revival of racism, misogynism, elitism, and military and national chauvinism. Its victims were

Jews, Communists, Social Democrats and libertarians of all kinds—and, finally, the nascent women's movement.

In America the period from World War I to the sixties was characterized by a successive revival of anti-Negro racism, anti-Semitism, the destruction of the American Left, and finally the cold war militarization of society based on a fanatic anti-Communism. In this same period a continuous reactionary pacification of the women's movement deprived women of many of their earlier gains in educational and professional fields.

This modern backlash against the libertarian tradition seeks to reinstate attitudes and social relations whose psychic roots run back through the Judeo-Christian and Classical cultures into the very foundations of civilization-building. The cry for liberty, equality and fraternity challenged the roots of the psychology whereby the dominant class measured its status in terms of the conquest of classes, nations, races and nature itself.

Lewis Mumford, in his monumental work on the foundations of ancient civilization, *The Myth of the Machine,* and its supplementary volume on modern technological society, *The Myth of the Machine: The Pentagon of Power,* has shown how civilization has been founded on a subjugation of man to machinery. A chauvinist, paranoid psychology has directed men's productive energies into destruction rather than the alleviation of the necessities of all, thus aborting the promise of civilization. The subjugation of the female by the male is the primary psychic model for this chauvinism and its parallel expressions in oppressor-oppressed relationships between social classes, races and nations. It is this most basic symbolism of power that has misdirected men's psychic energy into the building of the Pentagon of Power, from the pyramids of ancient Egypt to the North American puzzle-palace on the Potomac.

The psycho-social history of the domination of women has not been explored with any consistency, so the effort to trace its genesis and development here can only be very general. However, it appears that in agricultural societies sexist and class polarization did not immediately reshape the religious world view. For the first two millennia of recorded history, re-

ligious culture continued to reflect the more holistic view of
society of the neolithic village, where the individual and the
community, nature and society, male and female, earth goddess
and sky god were seen in a total perspective of world renewal.
The salvation of the individual was not split off from that of
the community; the salvation of society was one with the renewal of the earth; male and female played their complementary roles in the salvation of the world. This primitive
democracy of the neolithic village persisted in the divine pan-
theons of Babylonia, despite the social class stratification that
now appeared.

In these early civilizations this holistic world view was expressed in the public celebration of the new year's festival,
wherein the whole society of humanity and nature experienced
the annual death of the cosmos and its resurrection from pri-
mordial chaos. In this cult the king, as the personification of the
community, played the role of the god who dies and is reborn
from the netherworld. His counterpart was a powerful feminine
figure who was at once virgin and mother, wife and sister, and
who rescued the dying god from the power of the underworld.
The king united with her at the end of the drama to create the
divine child of the new year's vegetation. The crisis and rebirth
encompassed both society and nature: the hymns of rejoicing
celebrated the release of the captives, justice for the poor and
security against invasion, as well as the new rain, the new
grain, the new lamb and the new child.

Somewhere in the first millennium B.C., however, this communal world view of humanity and nature, male and female
carried over from tribal society started to break down and the
alienations of civilization began to reshape the religious world
picture. This change was partly aggravated by the history of
imperial conquest that swept the peoples of the Mediterranean
into larger and larger social conglomerates where they no longer
felt the same unity with the king, the soil or the society.

The old religions of the earth became private cults for the
individual, no longer anticipating the renewal of the earth and
society but rather expecting an otherworldly salvation of the

individual soul after death. Nature itself came to be seen as an alien reality, and men now visualized their own bodies as foreign to their true selves, longing for a heavenly home to release them from their enslavement within the physical cosmos. Finally, earth ceased to be seen as man's true home.

Hebrew religion is significant in this history as the faith of a people who clung with particular tenacity to their tribal identity over against the imperial powers of civilization. Hebrew society inherited kingship and the new year's festival of the temple from their Canaanite neighbors. But Yahwism repressed the feminine divine role integral to this cult and began to cut loose the festival itself from its natural base in the renewal of the earth.

This desert people claimed the land as a divine legacy, but they imagined a manner of acquiring it that set them against the traditional cult of the earth. They took over the old earth festivals but reinterpreted them to refer to historical events in the Sinai journey. The messianic hopes of the prophets still looked for a paradisal renewal of earth and society, but this renewal broke the bonds of natural possibility and was projected into history as a future event.

So the pattern of death and resurrection was cut loose from organic harmonies and became instead an historical pattern of wrath and redemption. The feminine imagery of the cult was repressed entirely, although it survived in a new form in the symbol of the community as the bride of Yahweh in the Covenant. But the bride was subordinate and dependent to the male Lord of Hosts who reigned without consort in the heavens, confronting his sometimes rebellious, sometimes repentant people with punishment or promises of national victory.

The hopes for a renewal of nature and society, projected into a once and for all historical future, now came to be seen as less and less realizable within history itself. And so the prophetic drive to free man from nature ended in the apocalyptic negation of history itself: a cataclysmic world destruction and angelic new creation.

In this same period of the first millennium B.C. we find in

Classical philosophy a parallel development of the alienation of the individual from the world. Like the prophets, the philosophers repudiated the old nature gods in their sexual forms of male and female divinities, and maleness was seen as bodiless and intellectual.

For Plato the authentic soul is incarnated as a male, and only when it succumbs to the body is it reincarnated in the body of a female and then into the body of some beast resembling the evil character into which it has fallen. The salvation of the liberated consciousness repudiates heterosexual for masculine love and mounts to heaven in flight from the body and the visible world. The intellect is seen as an alien, lonely species that originates in a purely spiritual realm beyond time, space and matter, and has been dropped, either as into a testing-place or through some fault, into this lower material world. But space and time, body and mutability are totally alien to its nature. The body drags the soul down, obscuring the clarity of its knowledge, debasing its moral integrity. Liberation is a flight from the earth to a changeless, infinite world beyond. Again we see the emergence of the liberated consciousness in a way that alienates it from nature in a body-fleeing, world-negating spirituality.

Christianity brought together both of these myths—the myth of world cataclysm and the myth of the flight of the soul to heaven. It also struggled to correct the more extreme implications of this body-negating spirituality with a more positive doctrine of creation and incarnation. It even reinstated, in covert form, the old myths of the year cult and the virgin-mother goddess.

But the dominant spirituality of the Fathers of the Church finally accepted the anti-body, anti-feminine view of late antique religious culture. Recent proponents of ecology have, therefore, pointed the finger at Christianity as the originator of this debased view of nature, as the religious sanction for modern technological exploitation of the earth.

But Christianity did not originate this view. Rather it appears to correspond to a stage of development of human consciousness that coincided with ripening Classical civilization. Christianity took over this alienated world view of late Classical civilization, but its oppressive dualities express the basic alienations at work in the psycho-social channelization of human energy since the breakup of the communal life of earlier tribal society.

What we see in this development is a one-sided expression of the ego claiming its transcendental autonomy by negating the finite matrix of existence. This antithesis is projected socially by identifying woman as the incarnation of this debasing threat of bodily existence, while the same polarized model of the psyche is projected politically upon suppressed or conquered social groups.

The emphasis upon the transcendent consciousness has literally created the urban earth, and both abstract science and revolution are ultimate products of this will to transcend and dominate the natural and social world that gave birth to the rebellious spirit. The exclusively male God who creates out of nothing, transcending nature and dominating history, and upon whose all-powerful wrath and grace man hangs as a miserable, crestfallen sinner, is the theological self-image and guilty conscience of this self-infinitizing spirit.

Today we recognize that this theology of rebellion into infinity has its counterpart in a world-destroying spirituality that projects upon the female of the race all its abhorrence, hostility and fear of the bodily powers from which it has arisen and from which it wishes to be independent. One can feel this fear in the threatened, repressively hostile energy that is activated in the dominant male society at the mere suggestion of the emergence of the female on an equal plane—as though equality itself must inevitably mean *his* resubjugation to preconscious submersion in the womb.

This most basic duality characterizes much recent theology. Karl Barth, despite his model of co-humanity as the essence of the creational covenant, insists on the relation of super- and sub-ordination between men and women as an ordained necessity of creation. "Crisis" and "secular" theologians such as Bultmann and Gogarten continually stress the transcendence of history over nature, defining the Gospel as the freedom of the liberated consciousness to depart endlessly from natural and historical foundations into the contentless desert of pure possibility. Such theologians are happy to baptize modern technology as the expression of the freedom mediated by the Gospel to transcend and dominate nature.

Today, both in the West and among insurgent Third World peoples, we are seeing a new intensification of this Western mode of abstractionism and revolution. Many are convinced that the problems created by man's ravaging of nature can be solved only by a great deal more technological manipulation. The oppressed peoples who have been the victims of the domination of the elite classes now seek to follow much the same path of pride, transcending wrath, separatism and power in order to share in the benefits of independence and technological power already won by the dominant classes.

Yet at the same time, nature and society are giving clear warning signals that the usefulness of this spirituality is about to end. Two revolutions are running in contrapuntal directions. The alienated members of the dominant society are seeking new communal, egalitarian life styles, ecological living patterns, and the redirection of psychic energy toward reconciliation with the body. But these human potential movements remain elitist, privatistic, aesthetic and devoid of a profound covenant with the poor and oppressed of the earth.

On the other hand, the aspirations of insurgent peoples rise along the lines of the traditional rise of civilization through group pride, technological domination of nature and antagonistic, competitive relationships between peoples. Such tendencies might be deplored by those who have so far monopolized technology and now believe they have seen the end of its fruitfulness, but they must be recognized as still relevant to the liberation of the poor and oppressed from material necessity and psychological dependency.

We are now approaching the denouement of this dialectic. The ethic of competitiveness and technological mastery has created a world divided by penis-missiles and counter-missiles that could destroy all humanity a hundred times over. Yet the ethic of reconciliation with the earth has yet to break out of its snug corners of affluence and find meaningful cohesion with the revolutions of insurgent peoples.

The significance of the women's revolution, then, may well be its unique location in the center of this clash between the contrapuntal directions of current liberation movements. Women are the first and oldest oppressed, subjugated people. They too must claim for themselves the human capacities of intellect, will and autonomous creative consciousness that have been denied them through this psychosocial polarization in its most original form.

Yet women have also been identified with nature, the earth and the body in its despised and rejected form. To simply reject this identification would be to neglect that part of ourselves we have been left to cultivate and to buy into that very polarization of which we have been the primary victims. The significance of our movement will be lost if we merely seek valued masculine traits at the expense of devalued feminine ones.

Women must be the spokesmen for a new humanity arising out of the reconciliation of spirit and body. This does not mean selling short our rights to the powers of independent personhood. Autonomy, world-transcending spirit, separatism as the power of consciousness-raising, and liberation from an untamed nature and from subjugation to the rocket-ship male— all these revolutions are still vital to women's achievement of integral personhood. But we have to look beyond our own liberation from oppression to the liberation of the oppressor as well. Women should not buy into the masculine ethic of competitiveness that sees the triumph of the self as predicated upon the subjugation of the other. Unlike men, women have traditionally cultivated a communal personhood that could participate in the successes of others rather than seeing these as merely a threat to one's own success.

To seek the liberation of women without losing this sense of communal personhood is the great challenge and secret power of the women's revolution. Its only proper end must be the total abolition of the social pattern of domination and subjugation and the erection of a new communal social ethic. We need to build a new cooperative social order out beyond the principles of hierarchy, rule and competitiveness. Starting in the grass-roots local units of human society where psycho-social polarization first began, we must create a living pattern of mutuality between men and women, between parents and children, among people in their social, economic and political relationships and, finally, between mankind and the organic harmonies of nature.

Such a revolution entails nothing less than a transformation of all the social structures of civilization, particularly the relationship between work and play. It entails literally a global struggle to overthrow and transform the character of power structures and points forward to a new messianic epiphany that will as far transcend the world-rejecting salvation myths of apocalypticism and Platonism as these myths transcended the old nature myths of the neolithic village. Combining the values of the world-transcending Yahweh with those of the world-renewing Ba'al in a post-technological religion of reconciliation with the body, the woman and the world, its salvation myth will not be one of divinization and flight from the body but of humanization and reconciliation with the earth.

Our model is neither the romanticized primitive jungle nor the modern technological wasteland. Rather it expresses itself in a new command to learn to cultivate the garden, for the cultivation of the garden is where the powers of rational consciousness come together with the harmonies of nature in partnership.

The new earth must be one where people are reconciled with their labor, abolishing the alienation of the megamachine while inheriting its productive power to free men for unalienated creativity. It will be a world where people are reconciled to their own finitude; where the last enemy, death, is conquered, not by a flight into eternity, but in that spirit of St. Francis that greets "Brother Death" as a friend that completes the proper cycle of the human soul.

The new humanity is not the will to power of a monolithic empire, obliterating all other identities before the one identity of the master race, but a polylinguistic appreciativeness that can redeem local space, time and identity. We seek to overcome the deadly Leviathan of the Pentagon of Power, transforming its power into manna to feed the hungry of the earth. The revolution of the feminine revolts against the denatured Babel of concrete and steel that stifles the living soil. It does not merely reject the spirit-child born from the earth, but seeks to reclaim spirit for body and body for spirit in a messianic appearing of the body of God.

Chapter 9

Is There a Black Theology?
The Validity and Limits
of a Racial Perspective

The black church is the oldest institution of Black Power and the cradle of the modern theology done in the context of the black experience. Yet the black church has been somewhat late and ambivalent in responding to the cry for a Black ideology for the black movement. Part of this ambivalence is a reflection of the weakness of the black church, to be sure; a reflection of its subservient status in the white society, but a part of this ambivalence may reflect a deeper instinct; a sense that the character of black ideologies at the present time goes against the grain of the deep commitment of the black church to a black liberation in the context of a full human liberation. It is this validity, but also these limits to the black perspective for theology that will be sketched in this essay.

The black church is the nursemaid of Black Power. In the days of slavery and through the dark period of reaction after Reconstruction, the black church was the one institution owned and run by the black community. Black autonomy was pioneered by the black church when it broke from the white denominations to form autonomous black denominations. The church was often the only building owned independently by the black community, and so it naturally became the center of its social and political life as well. The minister remains even today the political and social leader of the black community. When I was in Mississippi in 1965, almost all the Head Start programs sponsored by the independent Child Development Group of Mississippi were in black churches. It was in black churches that rallies and meetings were held and from black churches that the demonstrators marched out to confrontations in the streets and courthouses, singing the "soul" anthems of black Christianity. When Stokely Carmichael proudly boasts that the black community is the only place in America where people call each other "brother" and "sister," he is pointing to a heritage of the black church from the communitarian tradition of the Radical Reformation.

But, like the black community, the black church has been ambivalent in its heritage. It has imitated the styles of white Christianity. It has often suppressed its indigenous musical tradition for the more "proper" style of the white church. It has largely failed to bring art from black people into the churches. The pictures in the Sunday school books and the Biblical figures that paraded down the walls and the stained glass windows were uniformly Caucasian in features and coloring. There was little sense of the incongruity of this, not only for the self-image of the worshipers, but in terms of Biblical history itself! In short, the black church, as an expression of a suppressed people, has often overvalued the dominant culture and undervalued and even despised its own traditions and self-expression.

The cultural aspect of Black Power is an effort to reclaim and cultivate a culture in the context of the Black experience where the black person can recover his own soul from alienation. This cultural revolution must create a deep transformation in the style of the black church which will revive much of what is old and buried, but transform this into a new key for an age of new militancy. The black seminary, such as the one in which I teach at Howard University in Washington D.C., surely must be the creative center for the evaluation of the validity and limits of this new culture of blackness in a theological perspective.

In what sense is a black theology a possible form of the Christian Gospel? How does one combat the ready cry that such an idea must necessarily be a reverse form of the racist ideology which has been practiced all too long in the white churches, to assure their members that the separation and superiority of the white race is "in the Bible" and expresses the "will of God"? Is black theology just a new form of racial propaganda, making Christ in the image of black exclusivism, just as the whites made Christ in the image of their exclusivism? I believe that black theology walks a razor's edge between a racist message and a message that is validly prophetic, and the character of this razor's edge must be analyzed with the greatest care to prevent the second from drifting toward the first.

First let me state that I believe that there is a black theology that is reconciling rather than alienating, catholic rather than racist, and which really restates the authentic message of the prophets within a black perspective. I will summarize a number of themes which such a black theology could treat with great power.

The characteristic of racism is that it puts the category "man" below the category of the particular racial group. The species becomes the mode for defining the authentic nature of the genus, so that everyone outside that group is defined as not truly "a man." This is true of every form of bigotry, whether it be that of race, culture, class or sex. The picture projected upon the "lower" group by the dominant society tends to be fairly similar. The rejected group is always pictured as passive, dependent, unstable, emotional, potentially vicious, subject to unrestrained passions, lacking in true intelligence and reasoning powers. All this is summed up in the conclusion that the group is not fully or truly "human."

The oppressed group internalizes this image and looks with contempt upon itself. Even its forms of sabotage of the power of the dominant society tend to be self-weakening, taking the form of that "laziness" that attempts to survive under the lash by appearing incompetent. The oppressor also is dehumanized by this false relationship, for he receives no authentic communication from the oppressive role, but receives back only a mask donned by the oppressed to reflect the demands of those in power. Revolt against this oppressive relationship then is really a demand for truth and order in an untruthful and disorderly universe. The "law and order" of the oppressor is a false order. The rebel against oppression is demanding a true order based on the common nature of all men. His rebellion then is a discovery and affirmation of his own humanity and a demand that the oppressor recognize his humanity on the same basis as he recognizes his own. Rebellion is the breaking of silence between man and man: the initiation of true communication for the first time, based on two autonomous selfhoods that can stand as "I" and "Thou" for each other. In rebellion the rebel affirms a common human nature as the ground upon which both he and the oppressor stand and the basis upon which the oppressor must recognize the justice of his demands. The oppressor is rejected as a master, but not as a man. This means that rebellion retains its just ground only when the limits of rebellion are observed; when the rejection of the inhumanity of the oppressor, on the ground of their common humanity, does not fall over into a rejection of the humanity of those who occupy a position of unjust power.

In his best selling book, *Soul on Ice* Eldridge Cleaver tells how he came to an existential realization of this truth, after first expressing his rebellion against white society by raping (symbolically murdering) white women. "I came to realize that I had gone astray, not so much from the white man's law, as from being human, civilized, for I did not approve of the act of rape." Commenting on this realization later, in his *Post-Prison Writings and Speeches,* Cleaver said, "I came to realize that the particular women I had victimized had not been actively involved in oppressing me or other black people. I was taking revenge on them for what the whole system was responsible for. As I thought about it, I felt that I had become less than human. I also came to see that the price of hating other human beings is loving oneself less."

An authentic black theology of liberation, therefore, would be very sensitive to this nature of authentic rebellion. It would be a demand for order over against systematized disorder and an affirmation of the humanity of all men as the context for affirming black humanity. Such a black theology would be catholic and humanistic, not racist. Yet its universality would not be abstract. It would take black humanity as the particular which it celebrates as the concrete place where the universal is being realized. This particularity would not contradict its universality, but would draw on the other side of Biblical theology; namely, its contextualism. Biblical theology is universal, but never abstract. The one God who is the Lord of all history and all men always addresses himself to man in his concrete historical situation. Biblical particularity is not exclusive, but contextual. The God who is One, presides over all men and histories by addressing each community and person where it really is.

For this reason the encounter of man with God is not couched in abstract philosophical terms, but takes the forms of the particular historical circumstances in which a people experiences the revelation. A black theology would be contextual, but not exclusive or racist. It would take the particular historical experience of the Afro-American as the unique context in which God addresses us here and now and the Gospel is proclaimed. Since this experience of the Negro in America cannot be discussed without talking at the same time with how he has experienced the reality of whites, a black theology would not be addressed merely to black people, but would be as much an illumination of the white situation as well.

Because the Afro-American experience is inseparable from its interaction and shaping by white America; i.e., the Black experience has been primarily the Black experience *of* White America, a theology done in the context of the Black experience would act as a paradigm of the fall and redemption of man in terms of their relational structure to each other. In Biblical theology the relation between man and man is a paradigm of the relation between man and God. Man expresses his relation to God through his relation to his brother. Apart from his relation to his brother there is no relation to God. As John 4:20 puts it, "he who says he loves God and hates his brother is a liar, for how can we love God whom we do not see, if we do not love our brother whom we do see?" Sin is broken rela-

tion to God, expressing itself in alienation and broken relationship with the brother; an oppressive power over the brother. Redemption is the overcoming of alienation and the restoration
of community with the brother, which expresses God's restored
community with us. This is the unbreakable triangle in the
Biblical sense of sin and reconciliation.

Black theology would be a potent instrument for revealing
concretely this relational structure of sin and redemption. From
the black experience in America, black theology would illustrate the many ways people oppress each other, and even feign
reconciliation in order to assert an oppressive relationship in a
new form; don mask upon mask to prevent true communication. The black man understands the infinite duplicities of
this oppressor-oppressed relationship, because he has been going to school on this subject for three hundred years. On the
other hand, when communication begins to be restored, and
men find themselves recognizing each other as brothers, this is
experienced as an event that goes beyond their immediate
situation and powers. It is a gift from beyond the black situation
or the white situation that one cannot argue oneself into, prove,
justify or earn. In such a fashion did Malcolm X find community
with white Muslims in the Near East and Eldridge Cleaver a
community with white radicals in Berkeley, not as something
that they expected, but as an unexpected breakthrough; a gratuitous surprise that gave each a new basis upon which to conduct the struggle.

Here then are some central themes for a Black theology.
From the black experience one sees concretely the meaning
of sin as alienation and broken community and redemption
as the new brotherhood discovered as grace. This is the meaning of the Church as the community of the New Humanity. The
themes of faith, and the nexus of man's struggle with God's
grace would find striking illustration through the black experience. A black theologian would draw upon the specific context and the historical experience of the Afro-American, revealed in all his cultural expressions, to reveal concretely the
meaning of the Biblical anthropology.

Other theological themes would also be revealed powerfully

through the black experience. A theology of power would be an important part of the agenda. Power is often seen as the epitome of the oppressive relationship; yet power is also divine. One speaks of God by saying "Thine is the Power." Power is man restored to his integrity and creativity, so that his actions directly and effectively express his soul. Power is participation in the making of one's destiny. Power is effective action. Power is the ability to create autonomously. Power alienated from this integrity becomes oppressive, but man's redemption is the restoration of human power from alienation to self-directed and self-fulfilling creativity. In such a fashion does Marxism speak of man's "fall" as his alienation from his "work," while the redeemed society would be one where man's alienation from his power is overcome, and his creativity restored to an integrated self in community with one's fellowmen and nature.

The cultural revolution demanded by Black Power is itself a demand for catholicity. The Gospel is not to be couched in terms of one people and one culture. God is the God of all men, each in his own particularity and culture. So the Gospel rightfully comes to the black man in the form of a Black Messiah, not in an exclusivistic, racist sense, but in the sense of that historical contextualism, which gives to each people a salvation that encounters their situation.

Black theology is also an affirmation of the goodness of creation. "Black is Beautiful" is a restatement of the Biblical doctrine of man. God looked at his creation in the beginning and "behold, it was very good." Each part was good in its own terms. There was no one standard of beauty to which all the rest of creation should bow in a debasing way. Each people then affirm their own particular integrity in affirming the beauty of the whole.

This however does not mean that things can be celebrated as they have now become, because the meaning of sin is that man, who was made beautiful, can make himself very ugly. As Eldridge Cleaver said: "Guns are ugly." The white man looked at the black man with blue eyes cold with murder and the black man perceived, not a man, but a "pig." And behold, it was very ugly. The black man, too, in his self-hatred and self-repudiation and his internalizing of the depreciation of the white man, became ugly. The cry "Black is Beautiful," then, is also a cry for redemption, a cry for the restoration of one's natural integrity against the debasement into which one has fallen.

Finally a black theology is a theology of revolution—of the radical renovation of society. It brings judgment upon the white system based on false principles. It demands its overthrow and the recreation of the world based on entirely different principles; a world where men can live in wholeness and brotherhood. Such a theology expresses the longing of Biblical hope for historical salvation. The hope for salvation is the hope for the coming of the Kingdom of God; the hope for a new man in a new world, where the oppressive structures of the present "world" have been revolutionized and a new era of peace, brotherhood and obedience to truth has dawned. This apocalyptic vision has always been central to black hopes, black preaching and black music. The longing for deliverance and the Promised Land are the very heart of Black Christianity. When black Christianity sent its sons and daughters into the street in protest, they carried the music expressing this hope with them as the heart of the struggle. No one perhaps expressed more eloquently this tradition of black preaching than Martin Luther King who always drew on the language of the prophets to express his life-long confrontation between Amerika, the land of broken promises and America, which must become anew the Land of Promise for white men and black men alike.

More recently new voices have arisen in the black community to express the mood of anger and militancy which arose with the frustration of this movement that held out, so prematurely, the palm of reconciliation to the white community, conditional upon some real show of good will. James Cone's recent books, *Black Theology and Black Power* and *A Black Theology of Liberation* are efforts to create a new black theological reflection in the context of this new mood of militancy and disillusionment with the willingness of the white man to respond to persuasion, short of violence. Cone identifies "whiteness" uncompromisingly with evil, and "blackness" with authentic humanity. Whiteness symbolized the demonic powers which hold mankind, personally and socially, in thrall to inauthentic existence. Blackness is liberation from this power and the resurrection of man. This dual identification turns upon a metaphor, but a metaphor which he insists on taking as a "contextual absolute" for our times in the United States of America. Whiteness here is oppression. Blackness is the oppressed who struggle for liberation. Whiteness is the incarnation of sin. It expresses exactly what Egypt, Babylon and Rome meant in the context of Biblical historical symbols. Whiteness is the oppressive power of the imperial society which defies its own image and blots out the face of the Living God; thereby demonizing the entire structure of human, social and historical existence. The Exodus people see themselves as pitted against this imperial power in a way that incarnates the theological conflict between fallen and redeemed existence. The Living God of the Bible is the God who leads mankind out of the slavery to whiteness through a path of suffering which is hope-filled because it is on the way to the Promised Land of reborn humanity. The Living God not only leads his people out of the hell of whiteness. He comes to destroy whiteness; to abolish its works and pomps and overthrow its evil dominion so that the true Kingdom of God can arise on its ashes. Christian love is not passivity in the face of evil. Christian love comes to the oppressor in the form of divine Wrath which overthrows its diabolic kingdom, root and branch, so that all mankind can rise from its oppressive power to that new being promised them from the beginning. This "Black" resurrection is given first of all to the black-skinned Chosen People, but, through them, it is extended to the gentiles, their white-skinned oppressors, who, through the black Israel, may find their false selves overthrown, in order to receive through the black man a resurrected and restored humanity. In this manner Cone translates the languages of prophecy and apocalyptic into the contemporary confrontation between white and black America.

The crucial question which must be asked about this translation of Biblical categories is this: To what extent has Cone reified the metaphor, so that a contextual identification of theological with racial categories becomes an absolute? Cone would insist that his identification is true here and now, and so he need not discuss any hypothetical situations where it might not be true, or where the places might be reversed. All such speculative questions are merely an illegitimate effort by white folk to get themselves off the hook and avoid confronting the demonic elements incarnate in white society in relation to black society. But is this reply sufficient? To what extent has Cone taken seriously the fact that there are many kinds and levels of oppression here and now: oppression of whites by whites; blacks by blacks, oppression between nations, classes, sexes? If his categories intend to stand for a universal anthropology, theologically discerned, then the racial metaphor must make clear that "blackness" refers to all oppressed people in every situation. The oppressor/oppressed relationship is not intrinsic to certain kinds of racial "natures," as a permanent racial identity. The word "black," indeed, could then not primarily refer to race at all, but rather stand as a counter-symbol to the self-sanctification of the dominant society, which always identifies itself with all that is pure and good (white), and ideologically identifies its own social group with universal and normative humanity.

A certain confrontationalist relationship between social groups which, in certain historical contexts, stands for theological antitheses, at least in a provisional way, is justified. Both the prophets and the Gospel make use of this type of historical experience to reveal theological dialectics. But it is essential to us today, who have inherited the false interpretation of this tradition, in Christian and American self-sanctification, to clarify the limits of its legitimacy. The identification is essentially theological; not sociological or racial. Authentic and inauthentic existence are universal human possibilities. They exist where they actually exist, and this dialectic changes its boundaries constantly and ultimately runs across each of our hearts. It can never be permanently reified as the identity of any one sociological or racial group, including that of the historical Christian Church. The rejection of inauthentic society can never be construed as the rejection of the *humanity* of those people. Rather it is a rejection of the false, demonic powers that *possess* them, but in the name of a community that lies buried beneath that alienating power. The rebel undermines the moral ground upon which his revolution stands, as soon he rejects, not the inhumanity, but the humanity of his oppressor. The result of this change of the stance of the rebellion will be only a reversal of the oppressor/oppressed relationship and not a new humanity.

Cone does occasionally suggest that the new humanity of blackness is a metaphor for a universal humanity available to all men. But his free use of language about killing the oppressor, rather than loving him gives the overwhelming impression that theological categories have been wedded to racial identities in such a way that denies the humanity, as well as the false power, of white people. He fails to clarify the limits of his contextual identification of whiteness with the demonic. He fails to distinguish between whiteness as an inauthentic power possessing white society and whiteness as the "nature" of white people.

Cone also fails to create a theology which is sufficiently "black" in a cultural sense, and so reduces the humanity of black people to a one-dimensionality. The doing of theology in the context of the black experience, as we have seen, is nothing new to the black church. The black church has always preached the Gospel in the context of the black experience. The difference between traditional black preaching and Cone's Black theology, however, is that such a black theology becomes possible only when a Negro intelligentsia has arisen which has become divorced from the culture of the black community and has been educated in a white milieu. From this background the black intellectuals find it necessary to *reidentify* with a community from whose culture they have become alienated and in which they no longer live. Cone represents such a black intelligentsia in theology. His black theology differs from black preaching in that it finds it necessary to focus the categories of a white theology back upon the black community in a theoretical reidentification, whereas black preaching faced outward in the living context of the black community in a self-affirmation that was unselfconscious and universalistic. Cone was trained in an abstract German theology from whence he seeks blackness, whereas black preaching stood in a living relation to black culture and, from its milieu, preached universal brotherhood. The result of this reversal in the thought of a man like Cone is that his "blackness" and "whiteness" are peculiarly flat and "formal" in character. There is little living black culture reflected in Cone's sense of blackness. The heart of Black religion, in the Afro-American community, and its muffled echoes of African rhythms, might provide some real cultural alternatives to European theological categories. But these are lacking in the cultural background of Cone's theology. Cone's formal application of crisis theology to racial polarities results in a certain lack of "soul" in his theological charism, as though his theology did not arise from the living heart of a people weeping, shouting and singing their dilemma. If white people are more than oppressors, black people are more than the "oppressed."

Such a formal dialectic between white and black also fails to satisfy the Biblical concept of Election and Exodus. Israel was not the Elect people because they were oppressed. Israel's election does not rest on the fact of enslavement in Egypt or under the imperial powers, but upon the fact that they stand under the mandate of obedience to God, by which they themselves are judged, first of all. Cone's oppressor/oppressed dialectic offers no comparable concept of fidelity of the elect people to an intrinsic standard of righteousness, which would judge themselves, and not merely judge others. Rather, the righteousness of the black man becomes automatic, inherent in the situation of oppression as an "inalienable right." The white man becomes the irredeemable demon, while the black man becomes the unselfcritical "righteous one." The degeneration of conversation between black radicals and would-be sympathetic whites in recent years rests directly upon this kind of simplistic thinking.

Having sketched the nature and limits of racial polarities for a theology of liberation, the remainder of this essay will attempt a schematic presentation of the *praxis* of liberation and reconciliation between whites and blacks who are living through this dialectical tension. The black-white relationship created by classic white racism was a systematic dehumanization of the black person, resulting in a dehumanization of the white person as well. Revolt against this oppressive relationship indeed breaks the silence that divides them, but the dialogue begins by first operating out of all the old misunderstanding and false presuppositions. The races must go through a process of evolution in respect to each other before they can arrive at a point where real communication becomes possible. The following sketches the basic stages of this evolution.

The white man lives enclosed in a racial myth designed to exclude the black man from his consciousness and to deny his existence. All his institutions are designed to keep him from having to focus on the presence of the black person. The black person, by contrast, while living a life excluded from the benefits of white society, lives constantly in the presence of whiteness as an occupying power and encompasses him.

The first breakthrough for the white man is to have this myth shattered and to come into a consciousness of the existence of the black man, of his own white guilt and responsibility to make reparations. With this discovery, he ventures into the black community in order to bring himself into closer contact with black people and to "see what he can do."

In this first stage he is still unconsciously governed by the myth of white superiority. He assumes that black people can be "helped" primarily by bringing them into white cultural patterns and institutions. Since white institutions, as the institutions of the dominant society, are much superior in resources, this is a natural mistake. Integration then assumed the white paternalism which never regarded black humanity as a value in its own right, but took white humanity as the standard of humanity as such, and sought to save black people by whitewashing them. It was this implicit paternalism (a paternalism inforced by the black middle class leaders of the Civil Rights Movement) that was rejected with the eruption of Black Power and the death of non-violence.

Many white liberals have never adjusted to the shock of that development. They continue to regard it as a retrogression, and they are unable to see its necessity from the standpoint of the black situation. There was, however, a segment of white liberals who did enter into that deeper questioning of whiteness posed by Black Power. These people began to realize that, if they were to relate authentically to the black community, they must enter into a real death experience themselves. They must peel themselves like an onion, layer by layer, of their white superiority complexes, even if this appeared to lead to an abyss where there was nothing at all about themselves that they could positively affirm. These people set out to be educated by the black community. They entered into the Black experience of themselves as the "blue eyed devil." They resolved to obliterate their own faces and still their own voices in order to take into their consciousness the black experience of them unmediated by their own self-justifications.

This was a profound and necessary experience. But it also gave birth to an aberration which I would call "white sycophancy." The white person readily aborted the depths of his own self-dying into a facile repudiation of everything white. At the same time he uncritically extolled everything black. From the myth of black inferiority, he swung to the myth of black superiority. Every word from black lips must be defended and extolled as profound insight. The black man was beyond criticism. His was a super-humanity and consciousness that would remake the face of the earth. The role of the white radical was to throw himself into the ranks of the revolution which the black man was leading, even if this meant putting the gun to his own head.

The white man was still looking for a way to be related to the black revolution. He was wistfully hoping for a kind of invitation to return to the "arm-in-arm" march with his "black brothers" that he had enjoyed in the halcyon days of the Civil Rights Movement, although, to be sure, on terms that the black man would now define. He assumed that he would receive the return invitation at that point where he had reached a sufficient degree of radicalization and self-purgation of all things white. He sought acceptance by imitating and parroting the diatribes of Black Power.

This path was a delusion. The black man instinctively recoiled from the radicalized, alienated white youth. He recognized him to be filled with a strange self-hatred and to be making demands on the black community to provide him with an identity and purpose which had little to do with the authentic needs of the black community. The white radical's adoption of the stance of "white revolutionary in the Mother Country," far from bringing a new entente between the white and black movements, filled most black people with a deeper distrust of white youth, now reinforced by a certain contemptuousness.

This black dislike of the white radical movement was also mixed with ethnic and class feelings which the black community shares with ethnic, working-class America generally. As a rule the black radical has little ability to sort out his own legitimate objections to white radical expectations of the black community and his less legitimate feelings of inferiority and resentful inadequacy and his standard lower-class prejudices against "long hairs." What is legitimate in this dislike seems to me to be this: The white radical, alienated from his own community, was of little help to blacks. The black community needed to get itself together in a new self-image and to shake off white leadership images and authority figures. In this task white people might be of service in two ways; by providing supportive expertise to the black community that does not interfere with its own process of self-discovery: and by acting as radicals in the "establishment" to open up access to power to black people, and to be a mediator and translator of black demands to white power-holders. Black people are generally appreciative of those whites who are genuinely capable of acting as mediators, to push the unjust power of white society off the backs of the black community and to help transfer power to the hands of blacks. They are unappreciative of whites who wish rhetorically to co-opt blacks in some revolutionary scheme with little base in real possibilities.

The white liberal comes of age in the black community

when he learns how he can be of genuine service in this way; when he overcomes paternalistic and sycophantic relations to black people. This means that he confuses black people neither with the devil nor the Messiah. He recognizes them simply as people; men who are as much scarred by their historical experience as he is by his, and who have many psychological hangups as a result that they are painfully working through. The white person comes to the point where he can realistically and sympathetically recognize the faults of black people without this either reinforcing his superiority complex or "shattering his idealism." Rather, he dedicates himself all the more to the welfare of the black community, in understanding of—and solidarity with—its great gifts and its great wounds. Therefore he begins to become human in the black community and to be of service to human life there.

The black man is also going through painful stages of growth. This development I cannot sketch with the same inside authority, but I will try to give an account of it as I understand it. Unlike the white man, the black man is never out of the presence of the opposite community. Even in the sanctuary of his home, it surrounds him like strangling claws that grip all aspects of his life and creep into his very soul. He knows the white man well, the way a servant knows the secrets of a master's household, from the backstairs view. From this vantage point, he knows the faults of the white man better than the white man knows himself. This is true of all oppressive relationships. The oppressed must know the one he serves, but the oppressor, by disregarding him, knows nothing really about the oppressed. But the black man could never reveal his knowledge to the white man face to face. He has always to wear a mask that reflected to the white man the face which the white man projected upon the servant. This meant that the black man was a man who lived in feigned docility and repressed rage.

The first path open to him for his advancement was the path laid out by a strategy of feigned deference and suppressed rage. By imitating the white man, by deferring to his standards and by concealing his own perspective, he begins the torturous climb toward those benefits of culture, education and material goods offered by the dominant society. This path of deference is the one traditionally followed by the black middle class.

It is all too easy to overlook the remarkable achievements of this generation, amid the ready attack upon their evident limitations by their black sons today. This was a generation of Negroes who, under the most extreme handicaps, handicaps such as we can scarcely imagine today, pulled themselves up from the depths of impoverishment and ignorance, surmounted the revilement meted out to them from all sides, and obtained degrees in law, or medicine and some degree of economic security in the era of Jim Crow and mob lynchings. It was a hard discipline, and it taught the black middle class patience, gentility and a kind of modest insistence on their own self-respect. I believe that the achievements of this generation form the solid bedrock upon which the new militant is now building.

Even though they rudely discount the achievements of their parents in reaction against their limitations, the black militants today are predominantly the children of the black middle class. They are trying to reidentify with the black masses, but they stand on the shoulders of this achievement. Nevertheless, this ascent by way of the culture of deference and assimiliation to white presuppositions left a deep scar upon the black middle class. It forced the black man to hide his true feelings—even from himself. He could not admit his hostility, even to himself. It obliterated his own experience, his own soul, for he was constantly operating from the outside in, rather than acting spontaneously from the core of his own selfhood. Even his natural physical being must be denied; his skin lightened, his hair straightened, to make him look as indistinguishable from white society as possible.

It is these defects in the black middle class that the new generation explodes against. This explosion amounts to nothing less than a black cultural revolution. From the standpoint of this history of repression, Black Power is the resurrection of the black soul from the dead. It is a triumphant shout of joy at liberation from the cold chains of whiteness. Blackness is suddenly free to come out in the open. Hair sprouts with natural abandon. Black limbs leap and stretch in the sun. Above all, black rage tears off the mask and vents itself openly and honestly for the first time.

Yet, like all liberations, it takes time to spread the message, to consolidate it and to assimilate it into that solid sense of a common humanity which was one of the firmest convictions of the old black bourgeoisie. The assertion of Black Pride and Black Power readily spins off into the declaration of a community so exclusively defined by blackness that there is no commonality between black men and white men at all. The very possibility of communication between them is programmatically denied. The white person is not perceived in any way as an individual with his own chains and feeble good will. He becomes a walking symbol of historical crimes against the black race. It is, at this point, still gratuitous to speak over much about a "black racism." The racist presuppositions have been laid to be sure, but they cannot be activated, as long as the white power structure remains still intact and the blacks remain essentially dependent. Yet this is the crucial parting of the ways between a black movement, which will grow increasingly self-enclosed, or a black movement which might find in Black Power and Black Pride a new stance to communicate with whites on a real basis of mutual independence and equality. Whether this latter possibility is actualized depends on the complementary growth of our white man to the point where he is really willing to relinquish false power and to fight in a complementary way for the black community to help it to remove the foot of white power from its back. As Black Power grows to real independence and a sense of autonomy, and encounters whites ready to affirm that development, the two communities begin to reach a point where self-affirmation takes on the proportions of greater parity and justice, and where, for the first time, white people and black people, may begin speaking to each other, person to person, for the first time.

Chapter 10

Communitarian Socialism and the Radical Church Tradition: Building the Community of Liberation

In 1826 Robert Owen, the pioneering leader of utopian socialism, bought out the Rappite Christian pietist community of Harmony, Indiana, in order to use it as the site for his own projected socialist community of New Harmony. This little event is symbolic of a point of contact between utopian socialism and the radical Church tradition. The United States has long been fertile ground for utopian experimentation of both a religious and a secular kind, and, when the utopian socialists of the nineteenth century looked for territory in which to test their social theories, it is not surprising that they turned to America, because it was here that utopian communities from the left wing of the Reformation still flourished. Indeed one of the ironies of this relationship was that the Christian utopias often proved more prosperous than the socialist ones, and socialist theoreticians toured the thriving communities of the Shakers and Rappites in the second quarter of the nineteenth century to find out how, on a practical level, socialist communities worked.

Robert Owen thought of himself as anti-religious, but there

was more than a streak of the old English Christian millenarianism in his personality. In common with others of the radical socialist tradition, such as Fourier, San Simon and Kropotkin, he thought of his own doctrine as a "new" religion, or perhaps the authentic Christianity. But he set his face against the established Church, which he saw as the bulwark of the propertied classes. He particularly rejected the doctrine of the depravity of man central to English Puritanism, which he saw as the theological mainstay of the upper classes, robbing the common man of faith in his human potential. Left wing leaders of the radical Reformation in the sixteenth century similarly contended against the magisterial Protestant doctrine of the depravity of man and the bondage of the will. Anabaptist theologians stressed the radically fallen church and society, but placed their faith in the freedom of man to make a radical break with these corrupt social conditions and to place his life in the service of the good in a transformed human community. On a less theological level, Robert Owen also saw the root of evil as lying in corrupted social conditions, rather than in an irredeemable flaw in man himself.

Like the Christian radicals of the Reformation period, the utopian socialists did not believe in waiting for some radical renovation of the universe from on high to begin their own experimentation. They saw themselves as already the avantegarde of a new humanity that was beginning, even if in a small way, to create the redeemed pattern of human life that was to be the pattern of life in the Kingdom of God. Both Christian and secular utopianism look forward to a renovated humanity in a future messianic age, but believe that they can begin to develop this pattern in a provisional way in experimental communities here and now. This view contrasts with Marxist socialism (similar to Puritanism) which argued that it was impossible to build the future messianic society now or even project what its pattern of life might be. Rather, one must concentrate on destroying the political structure of the old society, using the "elect" as a political party, and, when the final cataclysm occured, the new society would form itself according to the historical conditions that would arise after the Revolution.

Left wing socialists rejected Marxists on this crucial point, for they recognized that there must be a harmony between the means and the ends of the Revolution. One cannot build a "peaceable kingdom" with the sword, nor the classless society with an authoritarian party. Rather, the life style, organization and methods of the revolutionaries would determine the pattern of the society which would arise after the Revolution. So the revolutionary process itself must be seen as, not just the struggle to put an end to the old world, but the provisional beginning of the new world. If the Revolution is really to bring about a communitarian society, the revolutionary must begin to live that new communitarian society now, in his revolutionary life style and methods.

Like the Christian radicals, communitarian socialism was born in a radical rejection of the state. But it also rejected the hierarchical organization of the revolutionary party (church). This may surprise many Americans who have become accustomed to thinking of socialism as the collectivization of property under the centralized control of an all-powerful state. But this kind of state socialism contradicts the original socialist vision. Even Marxism preserves the original anarchist thrust of socialism, in the belief that the dictatorship of the proletariat will only be a brief transitional period of social reorganization that will be quickly superceded by the "withering away of the state." The ultimate socialist vision was an anarchist one, where alienated and oppressive authority on all levels was overcome, and man is to be reintegrated into direct control of his own political, economic and social processes. Here again left wing socialists differed from Marxists, because Marx believed that, although the ultimate communist society is to be "stateless," the revolutionary process itself must work through political organization. But the left wing socialists saw this method as selling out the revolutionary goal. A revolution made through an authoritarian political party cannot yield an anarchist future society, but rather the political organization and methods of the party would itself become the new ruling class of the revolutionary state. This is why Bakunin so vehemently contested the political methods of Marx within the First Internationale, and Kropotkin and others, even many who thought of themselves as Marxists, such as Rosa Luxemberg, deplored the centralized dictatorial party structure of Lenin.

Like the radicals of the Reformation, left wing socialism was "congregational." It believed in a social structure decentralized to the local community level. Each community would be autonomous. Work should be scaled down to the human level, and technology would be measured by human needs and humanizing functionality, rather than human functions being pressed into the service of a technological logic. On this level utopian and anarchist socialism represents an early revolt against the social organization that industrialization and technology regard as "efficient." Indeed, there was a real element of primitivism in radical socialism which wished to revive in a utopian manner the pre-industrial communitarianism of the feudal village, which was being obliterated in Europe wherever the industrial revolution spread. Left wing socialism was idealistic about a peasant life in France and Russia, and saw the patterns of communal life and land ownership, shared work and handicrafts, still preserved there, as the base from which to build the new socialist community. On the same ground, they also cultivated such Christian utopians as the Hutterites, Shakers, and Rappites, who also preserved, in a rationalized and religious form, the lineaments of the preindustrial European village.

Yet there was more than just a reactionary character to the protest of radical socialism against technology and the state. Essentially it also foresaw that the modern technological state would be dominated by a dehumanized logic, in which human processes and needs would be subordinated to the processes and "welfare" of the machine. A machine logic rather than a personalist logic would control the form and priorities of the industrial state. Man would be subordinated to production, rather than production a tool tempered to personalist processes and goals. This subordination of man to machinery is indeed the very essence of modern industrial civilization, and left wing socialism raised an early and enduring protest against it. Essentially what radical socialism wanted was a use of technology that would remain scaled to human size, where it could remain tied to personalized modes of functioning. The factory would be owned in common by a local community which would communally make all the decisions about its management. Political authority also would remain on the level of the local community, where a man could directly represent himself in the primary forum. Participatory democracy would have been a congenial slogan for radical socialism. In the local community directly running its own political affairs, managing its economic life for its own welfare, alienation between individual and society, between work and life, between authority and freedom would, hopefully, be overcome. Man, in a direct relationship with nature and his socio-economic base, would be in charge of his own destiny. This, in Engels' language, would be the "ascent from the Kingdom of Necessity to the Kingdom of Freedom." Left wing socialists envisioned some kind of federalism, a common bank and a common market, that would link the autonomous communes together. But power over economic and political decisions would remain on the local level.

The Israeli kibbutz is perhaps the outstanding example of the social and economic application of this tradition, although it dropped the political autonomy of original anarchist socialism. The Soviets and the farm collectives in Russia, and the communes of China are also expressions of this same socialist principle, often building directly upon the preindustrial peasant communism of these areas, even though Marx himself originally had no use for such peasant socialism. The syndicalist tradition, which continues to be powerful in Latin American socialism, as well as in Spain, France and Italy, and partially reinstated in Titoist Yugoslavia, also springs from this left wing tradition which seeks communal ownership and management of the factory by the workers themselves (without the mediatorship of the Party). The IWW represented this syndicalist tradition in the United States. This libertarian, grass roots tradition of socialism was briefly revived in the French May Revolution of 1968 which especially pitted itself against the Leninist, party-dominated socialism of the Communists, as well as the hierarchical bureaucratism of the unions. Local control, participatory democracy in every sphere of activity, common ownership of the means of production by the workers themselves, without a mediating "party," abolition of all hierarchies, either dictatorial or "representational," and the shaping of technological processes to personalized functioning and purposes; these are the hallmarks of radical socialism. In this sense radical socialism rejects the social organization of so-called "capitalist" America and so-called "Communist" Russia equally. Both have sold man out to machinery.

In the 1890s, left wing socialists split into two distinct tendencies: the apocalyptic terrorist anarchism of Bakunin and the pacifist anarchism of Kropotkin. This split is remarkably parallel to the clash that rent sixteenth century Anabaptism between the militant apocalypticism of Thomas Müntzer and the Zwickau prophets, and the ill-fated Anabaptist revolution in Münster in 1535, and, on the other hand, the pacifist, quietist branch of Anabaptism, represented by the Brethern, Mennonites, Hutterites and, later, the Quakers who believed that the redeemed community should begin to withdraw from the dominant society to begin to build the "new world," but that they should not engage in violent struggle with the state. When Christ returned, then the present form of this world would be overcome, and the saints would inherit the new earth, but meanwhile they should cultivate their gardens, anticipating, but not preempting the avenging "Day of the Lord." For Münzter and the peasant radicals, however, that avenging Day of the Lord was already identified with their own movement, and so they felt justified in taking up the sword against the dominant society as cohorts of the warrior Christ of the Apocalypse, whose Last Judgment was beginning in their own flashing swords. Both Münzter and Bakunin were radical spiritualists and voluntarists. Terrorist anarchists who followed Bakunin rejected the deterministic historical materialism of Marx, who had declared that the Revolution only became possible through the ripening material conditions of the historical process. The anarchist terrorists, however, believed, that the Revolution did not wait upon this deterministic "kairos" of material conditions, but could be made at any time by those who had the will to rise up and set the example of total revolutionary rebellion to inspire the "masses." The spirit of man can dominate and reshape the material conditions and possibilities of society. This radical voluntarism and spiritualism are also characteristic of Maoism, as Robert Jay Lifton has shown (see his book on the Chinese Cultural Revolution and Mao, titled *Revolutionary Immortality*). This is doubtless one reason why Maoism attracts the new left, although its instinctive bias is toward radical rather than Marxist party socialism.

In left wing socialism, as also in the churches of the radical Reformation, one finds a radical pacifism and an apocalyptic violence erupting together. The provisional building of the "peaceable kingdom" and the sudden outbreak of the apocalyptic gesture mingle in these traditions, in their mutual relations and contradictions. Some, like Kropotkin, after some initial flirtations with violence, remained primarily committed to building the non-violent communitarian society, while others, such as Bakunin, Berkman and a host of lesser figures, acted out the apocalyptic gesture in terrorist confrontations with the state. Thus terrorism also had a distinct tendency to become entangled in a singular symbiosis with the police and the criminal underground, so that it often became difficult to distinguish anarchist from criminal. The police often became so thoroughly infiltrated into the anarchist movement that most of the anarchist "actions" became difficult to distinguish from the activity of police provocateurs! This too is a history that seems doomed to be repeated by New Left in America today!

In the last decade there has been a significant revival of the left wing socialist tradition in such advanced technological countries as the United States, Canada and France. At the same time, one also finds in Eastern European countries a desperate struggle against the Leninist-style Communist party, dominated by the Soviet Union. Czechoslovakia was the most notable recent example of the effort to reinstate a more independent, nationalist and humanistic socialism, against the Leninist-Stalinist party domination. On the other hand, in the Third World, one finds a new Marxism radically modified to meet pre-industrial, peasant conditions and nationalist, anti-

imperialist aspirations of non-European peoples.] It is difficult to sort out the contradictions of these various strands of
contemporary socialism, all of which wish to reassert the old
revolutionary hopes of socialism, but without the failures of the
old Left which seemed to do little more than create the centralized, technological state in a collectivized form. Marxism
itself has been beset by these contradictions from the beginning,
when it projected a classless society to be midwifed by an
authoritarian political party, and a new humanity liberated
from economic alienation to be generated by the acceleration
of industrialism. The importance of the left wing socialist
tradition has been less in its answers to these questions, than in
its continual raising of these questions, its resolute criticism of
the contradictions of the Marxist methods, and its clinging to
the original socialist communitarian, democratic vision.

In practice, Marxism has turned out to be, not the ideology
of advanced technological countries moving beyond the "highest
stage of capitalism to communism," as Marx thought it was, but
rather it has been adopted primarily by pre-industrial societies
as a way of making a rapid industrial revolution under authoritarian state control. It has become a tool for non-European or
colonialized people to catch the Western, technological fever,
but, at the same time, to revolt against Western domination.
Communism thus has become a part of the Westernization of
mankind, by which all nations follow the path of the technological, secularizing revolution carried out in the West these last
three hundred years. But, because the West went through this
revolution first, and then exported its superiority to underdeveloped countries in the form of colonialism and imperialism,
the industrial revolution in these areas must also take the form
of nationalist, anti-imperialist uprisings against the West. Thus
paradoxically Communism, itself a Western ideology, has become the ideology of anti-Western Westernization. The social
struggle in which the United States is locked in South East Asia
is largely due to our inability to understand the dialectics of
this revolutionary process.

Yet the achievement of this technological revolution on a
worldwide scale will only raise more insistently the post-

technological revolutionary questions with which Marx himself originally began. These are the questions which left wing socialism has always maintained as the central socialist vision, no matter how impractical these ideals might appear in practice. Bakunin's criticism of Marxism as an ideology which could only end in state capitalism under the new ruling class of the Communist party, rather than true, equalitarian socialism, has been more than amply borne out by the history of Marxist-Leninist states. Yet it is precisely in advanced technological countries (where Marx originally located his hope for the socialist revolution) that the questions posed by socialism about the humanization of technology and the scaling of the political and economic processes to personalist methods are suddenly newly relevant. This is even more so now that the very ecological fabric of the planet seems to be revolting against the violation of organic welfare and harmonies for technological methods and goals. Yet the achievement of the ideals of communitarian socialism in a new stage of society beyond advanced technological capitalism seems more puzzling than ever, even as the need for such a development seems the more imperative for human survival. For the first time world annihilation becomes a practical possibility and not just a wrathful vision. To find a human way into this perilous future, it seems imperative to find a social reordering where man can reconcile his technological ambitions and capacities with an ascetic temper, newly in tune with the earth, that can accept in a new way the finitude of the human project.

Although the New Left in America is highly volatile, there seems to me that, here and there, there is emerging a new way of combining the ideals and methods of communitarian socialism with a non-sectarian relationship to conventional society which can have some practical effect on its power politics. The New Left, like the radicals of the past, has been plagued by three tendencies which seem to pull in opposite directions and which seem impossible to reconcile: (a) the need to project a communitarian life style among a separated group, (b) the need to act directly to express its protest, unhampered by the political channels of conventional power politics, (c) the need to be practically useful, using organizational and communication tactics which can connect with and influence the conventional political structure. In recent years the Left can be seen splintering into factions over the inability to reconcile these disparate demands.

But gradually there is emerging a form which may combine these different desiderata in a functional way. The new "work-collectives" are groups devoted to building a new humanity which will reflect communitarian principles. They struggle to create a community which will reflect equalitarian and personalist human relationships, abolish hierarchalism, politically and sexually, and begin also to explore an ecological life style suitable for a non-exploitive relationship with nature. But they seek to modify conventional society by remaining in its midst. The commune thus operates as a supportive family for those engaged in direct political action, as well as a task force that engages in political organizing and communication around such direct action. The work-collective can also be a training center which spreads through spinning off groups to form new communities. There is both a closeness and a provisionality in the relationships which keep them from becoming closed "sects." New Left organizations today, of the kind that may be planning a "Spring Offensive" or running a Defense committee, or even acting as a research team, more and more, are organized as work communes. To run a "non-violent life center," as a group which is simultaneously a live-in commune, a task force and a training center, seems to be the central idea of numerous new groups and proposed groups which have come to my attention in recent months. Seminaries organized in this form also are being developed.

The interesting thing about this new form of the communitarian socialist tradition is its striking parallel to the radical concept of the relationship of the Church to society. The Church should relate to society, not by being co-opted by it to sanctify the *status quo,* nor simply withdraw from it in isolated purity, but rather the proper relationship of Church to society is dialectical. The Church should stand in the midst of conventional society, but not be "of it," but rather be the place where a significantly new humanity, functioning in a communitarian and non-exploitive way, is begun. Yet this new community also acts as a base to train its own members as a missionary force to preach the message, and convert "straight society" to new visions. The relationship between the two remains one of constant tension, and yet it must also be one of fruitful interaction, where concrete changes are being made in conventional society through the example and pressure of the prophetic alternative community. The prophetic community must also constantly poise itself against conventional society in order to renew its own life style and radical critique. There can be no final fusion between the two "until the Kingdom comes." Whether this is possible within finite history, or whether this goal acts as an inspirational reference which can never finally be incarnate in temporal structures, is an open question for both the Church and the radical socialist community, but the prophetic community must remain the place where the vision and radical demand of the Kingdom are constantly renewed and groups seek ever anew to find ways of living this vision as authentically as possible. Yet the radical community is not an end in itself, but it exists only for the sake of the "salvation of the world," and so it must also remain practically and pastorally related to conventional society, committing itself to concrete tasks of penultimate amelioration in order to advance, even by a little bit, the currency of love, hope and justice which can be lived in and through the social structures of mass society.

Chapter 11

The Dilemma of the White Left in the Mother Country

In 1957 Frantz Fanon, the Algerian psychologist and revolutionary thinker, wrote of the French Left:

> It must be pointed out that not a single attempt at an explanation is undertaken on the level of the population of the colonialist country. Because it has no hold on the people, the Democratic Left, shut in on itself, convinces itself in endless articles and studies that Bandung has sounded the death-knell of colonialism. But it is the real people, the peasants and the workers, who must be informed. Incapable of reaching the millions of workers and peasants of the colonialist people and of explaining and commenting on the realities of the drama that is beginning, the Left finds itself reduced to the role of a Cassandra. . . . The French democratic elements and intellectuals are familiar with the problem. Having seen it at close range and having studied it for a long time, they know its complexity, its depth and its tension. But all this knowledge proves futile because it is utterly disproportionate to the simple ideas current among the people.[1]

Fanon then goes on to accuse the French Left of a disguised paternalism toward the Algerian revolutionaries which mani-

157

fested itself in a consuming desire to advise and criticize the policies of the Algerians, while failing to face any concrete problems and refusing to immerse themselves in the political life of their own country. Thus the Left proves irrelevant and worse than irrelevant to the Algerian struggle because it failed to do the one thing that the revolutionaries needed it for, namely to focus back and communicate its position to the masses of the French people.

In a remarkably parallel passage, Sam Brown reports that in February of 1970 Madame Nguyen Thi Binh, the foreign minister of the Provisional Revolutionary Government of the NLF, remarked that she found student radicals very sectarian and reluctant to touch political power.

> She continued that the confused assortment of political objectives on the Left—from legalizing marihuana to overthrowing the government to providing free abortions—dilutes the political impact of the peace movement. The result, she suggested, is that the Vietnamese people and the American soldiers carry the burden of America's social problems. . . . I found these Vietnamese revolutionaries far more thoughtful than most young American revolutionaries. Their private conversation was radically different from their strident, ideological press releases, and they seemed to bear little malice toward the American people. They didn't express hatred for Middle America, or even for the soldiers in Vietnam. The negotiators seemed to be tough-minded realists, who expect a long war and don't believe that America is anywhere near collapse. In short, these communist leaders are very connected with reality, where political self-delusion can cost people their lives.
>
> One such delusion within the American peace movement has been the notion that we can retain a private dimension of political morality for ourselves.[2]

Sam Brown then goes on to argue that peace politics does not mean finding a sphere of disassociation from the American main stream where the radical can "witness" to his purity, but rather the psychologically and politically astute effort to reach Nixon's constituency and communicate to them a critical message in a tone and style that they can relate to, rather than one which needlessly turns them off from the content of the message.

I think it is not irrelevant to parallel these two views of the irrelevance of the Left in the colonialist country from a Third World revolutionary perspective, with the continued insistence of black people in America that the nostalgic desire of whites, however radicalized, to "play a role in the black movement" is to be rejected. The one thing concerned whites can do (and the one thing they never wish to do) is to go back and communicate their critical views to their own community. Hayward Henry, chairman of the first Congress of African peoples, meeting in Atlanta on September 3, 1970, when asked why whites and white newsmen were excluded from the Congress, said:

> Such deliberations are not conducive to the presence of whites. We are a family trying to solve problems together. The concerned whites must work with white people to eliminate racism.[3]

The dilemma of the "white left in the Mother country," stated quite simply, lies in its simultaneous alienation from and objective identification with the policies of the oppressor society. Its inability to find a constructive way of expressing this contradiction means that it embarks on a politics of personal alienation from its own society whereby it neither communicates with nor makes a realistic effort to make a political impact on its own society. It becomes a marginal group, locked into a conversation with itself, without access to the broader society which remain uninfluenced and even more confirmed in their own "simple ideas" by this alienation. To justify its radicalism, the Left turns to increasingly desperate ways of associating themselves with the revolutionary peoples, imitating their rhetoric, playing "guerrilla warrior." But here they again meet rebuff from the people with whom they seek to identify themselves, who insistently declare that they don't need a French or an American or a white ally for this kind of role, but rather for another role, the role of influencing his own people to back off the counter-revolutionary attack, and this is the role which the Left in the dominant society seemingly neither can nor will try to play in any effective way.

Is this a fair criticism? Surely there has never been such a large and vociferous Left in America as exists at the present time, and one which makes such an impact on the media. Yet its size, noise and impact seem matched by a peculiar impotence and frustration at every turn, while the actual political power slips increasingly to the Right, with the evident approval of a sizable majority of that part of the American people who can be reached by pollsters. In June of 1970 I attended the New Mobe strategy conference in Milwaukee which was intended to bring together the whole spectrum of the Left; communalists and Panthers, Peaceniks and Welfare Rights Mothers, Old Left and New Left, domestic concerns and Third World Revolutionaries. My overwhelming experience of this conference was that of a bankruptcy of both theory and programs, except for a vague commitment to participatory democracy in the running of conferences, which was productive of much shouting and general chaos in any attempt to create an agenda. A dynamism without outlet, every program, every line of argument having already been countered, one was left with a kind of tongue-tied rage. One group was a notable exception to this: the National Welfare Rights Organization, led by a formidable array of black women, with flying support troops of radical suburban women. NWRO was the only truly political, the only truly organized group at the conference. This was in such startling contrast to the rest of the assembly, that they themselves, on several occasions, declared their feeling of a need to hold back their own power lest they simply dominate the whole conference. Nevertheless, NWRO angrily rejected both radicals who were on their way to the country to cultivate their utopian socialist garden and those who were on their way to a long march to Washington to create cracked heads on the bridges and avenues of the Capitol. Both were politically irrelevant in their eyes. The message was plain. Unlike the other participants, NWRO was making a revolution for their own constituency, not for some other recipient of their bounty. Like the black and Third World revolutionaries cited above, they insisted that all the subtle rhetoric and ingenious activities of the white Left simply made no contact with concrete needs and any real strategy that might relate to those needs.

Any attempt to sort out this dilemma, it seems to me, must be based on some effort to make an objective analysis of where the revolutionary tensions in society, both in America and around the world, really exist, and what is their direction. Reducing this analysis to the simplest terms, we might say that there are two levels of revolutionary tension in the world which appear at cross purposes with each other. On the one hand, we have what I venture to call "conventional" revolutionary movements in the Third World and among deprived groups within developed countries. These movements result from a disproportionate development of the white Western countries, who went through scientific and technological revolutions in the seventeenth-nineteenth centuries which put them far ahead of the rest of the world developmentally, and then exported this technological superiority in the form of colonialism. This dominance continues in the form of economic neo-colonialism, buttressed by Western military power. The United States of America is today the prime representative of this economic-military neo-colonialism. In all fairness we should recognize that this role was partly thrust upon America, partly taken on in what was felt to be the purest philanthropy, but today all this operates as an elaborate obscurantism made the more impenetrable by Manichaean anti-communism.

Third World people basically want what we've got, but without our influence. They are fighting to equalize the goods and resources and technological development of the world, and this involves them in a struggle to throw off Western dominance and simultaneously to make a revolution of internal socio-economic development in their own country. This struggle, which is primarily a nationalist one, nevertheless links them up with Communism for two reasons. First, because communist states prove to be the states most sympathetic to this national and social struggle in practice, while Western nations are both the present and former colonialists and the counter-revolutionaries. Secondly, Communism, despite its original belief that it was the ideology of post-capitalistic society, has in practice, from the time of the Russian revolution, been primarily the vehicle for pre-industrialized states to make a rapid industrial revolution under authoritarian, centralized state control. That this contradiction between original Marxist theory and actual communist practice has produced all the obfuscation that presently dominates Marxist thought is true, but that is of less and less interest to Third World revolutionaries who are primarily interested in Marxism because it has some methods which work. But the loose pragmatic and basically nationalistic relationship to Marxism and other communist states among Third World revolutionaries presents only the more glaring contrast to the rigid ideological anti-communism of Americans especially, who insist on taking, in the most simplistic literal way, international, conspiratorial and atheistic rhetoric of an earlier Marxism which is largely irrelevant to how Communism is actually used in practice in revolutionary states such as Cuba and North Vietnam. In effect, by insisting that all communist states are necessarily under the dominance of a centralized world power centered in Russia and/or China, the USA often forces these states into a position where they have no alternative but to be so!

But this Third World, anti-colonial and internal developmental struggle is basically a conventional revolution that wishes to accomplish much of what the West has already accomplished, and, in the process, holds out the possibilities of a real world community of nations which are able to relate to each other on a more equal basis, instead of being dominated by a few advanced technological societies. Such struggles are well within our present competence and comprehension and take neither utopian nor millenarianist rhetoric to describe their intentions. Increasingly, nations around the world see the chief threat to world peace lying, not in these revolutionary struggles, but in the interventionalist policies of the United States. The USA has built up a militarized economic and political system that presently takes about 68 percent of the American budget. This military machine acts simultaneously as a counter-revolutionary force around the world and bleeds America itself dry, preventing any real movement toward solving America's own domestic problems of poverty, racism, decay of urban institutions and the like. The obvious conclusion is that this military machine must be drastically reduced, so that America can have funds to deal with its own domestic crisis, and be forced to back off its counter-revolutionary role in the rest of the world, so that, at least, development of under-developed nations and movements of national independence can go on in an inter-national sphere not so immediately dominated by American interests and so obscured by unrealistic fears and myths generated to support this American role. The one real role of the Left in the "Mother country" of the USA, then, is basically to do that job of political demythologizing in a way that can create a national consensus against this kind of inter-national role and militarization of the domestic economy.

Such a role of the Left is hardly, of necessity, one of revolution in America itself. Conceivably it could go on quite well within existing institutions. However, "undemocratic" in its processes, this society is uniquely a "mass" society, and if it has been pursuing the present policies, it has been because the vast majority of Americans have been persuaded that this is what they want and need. But this policy is not at all in their best interests, either domestically or in terms of international security. The greatest obscurantism of all takes place when we see basically the old liberal policies of centralism and internationalism, but without their previous social concerns and benefits, being sold to a Republican constituency under the name of old conservative values which originally spoke for exactly the opposite sentiments! It is obvious that the Left, if they had any real imagination and access to middle Americans, could make an enormous impact simply by working on the native conservative values of localism and anti-interventionalism and linking these conservative and deeply-held traits of mind of the American main stream with a sane and humane international policy. There are some politicians who can talk radicalism to the American working class with a conservative style. Others operate on an elaborate obscurantism of native American conservatism. Yet the Left, instead of demythologizing this obscurantism, continually creates rhetoric and tactics designed to play right into its hands! Nothing could be better for the Right than for the Left to posture, quite unnecessarily, as anarchists, communists and sex and drug freak-outs all at the same time, in the face of a terrified middle America, already deeply bred with visions of international communist conspiracy and the break down of moral values. The Left, year by year, since 1965, has been building up its symbiosis with the Right on lines that couldn't be better if they had been written by the CIA. The possibility of getting across the real messages that need to be communicated retreat farther and farther from the scene.

The second difficulty for the Left lies in the fact that we have two quite different levels of revolutionary tension going on simultaneously. The one level, which I have described, is the one I would call "conventional." It moves along the lines of nationalist and technological developments that have been taking place since the scientific revolution in the West in the seventeenth century. The second level is directed at this very scientific and technological revolution itself, and this struggle appears precisely in the advanced technological nations of the West themselves. Under the guise of new communalism, anarchism, new life styles, new forms of localism, and the recent alert to the ecological crisis, the ability of either the nature of man in his human relations or the organic nature of the world itself to support a mass technological society is being brought radically into question. This second level of revolutionary tension truly lends itself to utopian and millenarianist, and even apocalyptic thinking, because it is a revolution that we have not fought before, and we have no idea what its rules or direction may be. Ironically enough this is the revolution which is actually more closely in line with original Marxist thought of the sort that has been largely abandoned by communist states in practice. The confusion between these two levels of revolutionary tension which appear to be at counter-purposes with each other, accounts for much of the confusion of the white Left in advanced technological societies and their tendency, incomprehensible from the perspective of Third World people, to go off on drugs and free love and radical communes and imagine that thereby they are contributing to the efforts of the Viet Cong!

Having stated this problem in so elaborate and intractable a form, one must somehow offer, if not a "solution," at least a direction. The best I can seem to come up with by way of "direction" is simply to suggest that the radical has got to become a much more versatile fellow. He has got to recognize the imperative need for Third World, independent development and the disastrous threat of American military interventionalism, both around the world and at home, but he must also recognize that there is simply no short cut to changing this other than creating a new political consciousness among main stream Americans. It is here, in the political sphere, that these policies originated, and not in the military or at the draft boards, and this is where it must be changed. Only the most widespread, variegated and creative effort to get at the present mind-set of Americans which supports the present anti-communist paranoia, and to convince them of other options can finally touch this situation. Most of the present scenarios of the Left are either irrelevant or counter-productive to this process at the present time.

I have suggested that middle Americans have really been sold a bill of goods on their real interests that is counter to their own political philosophy. This fact, combined with the present awakening of a critical consciousness, helped along by the confrontation that is going on between the generations across the dinner tables all over America, offers a tremendous handle for such a new political coalition ready for real change, if the Left could learn to speak to it and lift it up into a broader understanding, instead of playing into a symbiotic polarization with it. But the radical, even as he seeks to engage himself in the most pragmatic and therapeutic relationship to American society on one level, must also remain very much a dreamer and a utopian, probing entirely new frontiers which are, as yet, unknown. For no sooner has a more just division of goods and political power been created in the community of nations around the world, than we shall all be caught up in the dilemma created by mass, technological society itself, and will have to search for quite new ways to curb and restructure technological development, so that it doesn't run counter to human and natural survival. Indeed there is good reason to believe that, for the Third World, if there is any hope of development at all, it cannot be done on the model of the West, but rather more on the order of development in China, which has combined both of these movements into one. More and more, what the Third World asks of the white radical in the Mother country is not to provide them with either the guns or the butter of the West, but simply to help them remove the stranglehold of the anti-development of the West from their throats so that they can find that root to grass roots development within their own means and powers that is called "liberation."

This mystification which appears to be endemic to the situation of the Left in the colonialist country expresses concretely the difficulties of mediating between history and transcendence that appears whenever society is in a process of critical social change. For this reason, this question and the contradictions that appear in society, that express both sides of the tension of change, are not unimportant for the theologian. For the theologian of liberation, who analyzes the question of "salvation" in a social and historical context, the contradictions and mystifications that appear in the struggle for social change are revelatory of all those same questions of human nature, grace, conversion and the "new being" which traditional theologians have analyzed in the context of individual "conversion."

The language of transcendence is essentially a language of "oughtness." When historical change is fused with a language of "oughtness," a value judgment is placed on the present and a future is projected that is intended to be some fundamental victory of right over wrong. It is typical of societies that derive from a messianic faith to think of social change in this way. Such a change in society requires a mediation between the existing order and some new possibility (as yet unclear) that can be only imagined and projected *vis à vis* the present order.

The process of social change thus requires an element of "new creation," bringing into existence possibilities that do not yet exist. The two sides of this historical dialectic are relative to each other at any particular moment. The "new" that is projected takes off by way of critique of the *status quo,* and is therefore shaped by it. Other problems go unnoticed in this process and may later appear in the new situation—an unavoidable limitation since history can only make relative, not absolute change.

Yet every period of profound crisis and demand for a "better world" opens up a vision of ultimate good as its final horizon and point of reference. And so every particular crisis becomes a moment for glimpsing a vision of absolute transformation of the "is" into the "ought" which is the standard of meaningfulness in human life. This utopian horizon is essential to the creativity and fertility of particular occasions of change. It is the grace that gives men power to strive for real change rather than one-dimensional alterations. Without this transcendent horizon men lack the imagination and vital spirit to seek really new possibilities.

Of course, this utopian horizon is fecund with self-delusions when applied literally. Yet without some element of hope that an ultimately better world can be built, no significant improvement in social life can take place. Though never completely incarnated in history (as we have known it), this hope is the ultimate meaning of every struggle for change, and no relative change comes about except through its mediating power.

In the actual scenarios of change, we find crucial interactions between various groups in structural situations that dictate differing roles in a dialectic. Let us define the "liberal" as the person who is sufficiently established in the present social system to have some power and influence within it, and yet is sufficiently open to the validity of the injustices being revealed to respond to the demand for change. The "radical," on the other hand, is the person whose consciousness has been sharpened by the struggle and who perceives that the demands of the times go beyond the conventional possibilities of change sanctioned by the existing system. This sensitivity to the "still more" beyond the present shape of the official culture is particularly sharpened by the disenfranchised, the victims of this culture. Through them, the radical becomes aware that to change their plight it will be necessary to alter drastically the presuppositions of the existing system itself, rather than merely making modifications within those presuppositions.

The radical may be an articulate member of this disenfranchised class or an alienated member of the dominant social group. In either case, he becomes a spokesman for the cutting edge of crisis and the need for historical transcendence. The radical is therefore the one who becomes most acutely conscious of the absolute horizon of the "ought" that is revealed in times of crisis, and he particularly becomes dissatisfied with partial solutions and struggles for the radically adequate way of incarnating this "ought." This involves him in some delusion, because this ultimate "ought" escapes the limits of historical finitude. But it also causes him to unmask any too-limited recognition of the "possibilities" and the tendency of those in power to create ideological blinders.

By its very nature, this polarized situation is replete with tendencies toward breakdown in communication. On the other hand, the liberal tends to hang on to his established position and to minimize the need or the possibilities for change. He cannot understand to what extent injustice has grown intolerable and anger uncontrollable. Secretly he believes that not much can be done, and wishes to do only that which will enhance his reputation as a "good guy" without any real risk to himself. So he fails to create the mediating connection between the present system and the changes that actually lie within his grasp.

The radical, in turn, grows increasingly frustrated and despairing as he perceives the extent to which urgent needs exceed the conventional operations, and recognizes the massive unwillingness of those in power—even those who claim to be "open"—to make an even partially adequate response. At this point he easily turns to alienated ways of acting out his sensitivity. But these, too, are only a more desperate way of trying to communicate with those in power.

By the nature of his position, the radical lacks power and access to lines of influence. So he seeks to make changes by acting outside the system. Sometimes, at moments when the disenfranchised actually do make up a majority of the population, he can create a new power base outside the old system. This is the kind of change perceived as "revolutionary." Yet it too is only relative change and necessitates the most *practical, political* use of power in order to succeed.

At other times, the social forces are too closely enmeshed in the present power system and, although the crisis may be no less acute and dangerous, a more complex process of change becomes necessary. Change must then be effected through interaction between those in power and those demanding reform and through a gradual conversion of large groups who are relatively established, but who come to see their deeper interests lying on the side of change. I think this is the current situation in America, and any useful strategy for change must connect realistically with this "material" basis. But this is also the situation where the breakdown of the mediating role of the liberal becomes most dangerous, and the possibility of a fascistic "turn to the right" may be the price of unrealistic radicalism.

Although superficially the responsibility for this breakdown lies with the radicals who turn to more alienated and alienating ways of expressing their dissatisfaction, it is too simple to make them the primary scapegoat. The real cause is the failure of the liberal, who remains silent, who fails to respond, who does not really believe that the need is so acute since it doesn't touch him personally. It is the liberal who is primarily responsible for the schism that opens up in the social dialectic, because he, who has some power and also some understanding of the need for change, fails to be dynamic and imaginative in creating a mediating force.

Consequently the radical, who is without access to power, feels himself increasingly overwhelmed by this non-response and intransigence. He comes to see all those in established positions as one monolith of "sin" and begins to look for alternative ways of making change. He may do this in quite realistic ways: there may be forces unnoticed by the existing system that can be gathered together "in the streets" and formed into a social force with the power to do the work of change the social leaders have failed to do.

Or the radical may express his desperation in ways that

are very little related to real political productivity and more attuned to personalistic acting out of his frustration and his rejection of the dominant society. Yet, even then, the "unrealistic" character of his tactics cannot be accurately judged by those in power, for the radical is acting on the edge of transcendence where no one can predict *a priori* what is realistic. This can only be discovered through the praxis that brings things into existence which were previously accounted "impossible."

As the struggle intensifies and the unresponsiveness of those in power increases the frustration of the dissenter, blowups occur. At this point the true colors of the liberal begin to show. Some liberals deeply sense the need for change and the justice of the cause of those who dissent, and the crisis motivates them to seek ways of responding more adequately. But there are others, previously identified with "liberal" sentiments, who quickly turn reactionary as the crisis intensifies and begins to touch their personal situation. These people have never really understood the plight of the oppressed. They have never sought to see and feel with their own humanity what oppression is all about, and they appear liberal only so long as it is safe and popular to do so.

One can spot the difference between authentic and pseudo-liberal reactionary liberals by their conversation and concern. If a liberal speaks not at all about the bombs the dominant society is using to devastate oppressed people, and instead concentrates in outraged tones on the occasional and ineffective outbursts of anger from the dissenters; if he is largely oblivious to the agony of poverty and oppression suffered by the victims of his society, but expresses overweening and punitive resentment at the violence or even inconvenience suffered by himself or one of his peers as a result of the frustrated radical scenarios in the streets; if, in short, he has no true sense of proportion of good and evil, magnifying the violence of a fringe group of dissenters but minimizing the violence that characterizes the daily relationships of the dominant society with its victims, then he is a reactionary, albeit in "liberal" colors.

This kind of failure to recognize the true proportions of good and evil should not be confused with direct criticism of the defects of dissent. A real liberal can be extremely critical of polarization and the role of the radical in this polarization, but he does not forget who is doing 99.9 percent of the violence and dehumanization in the world, and where the responsibility for the breakdown in communication lies. Therefore, while he regrets the blowups, he understands them as a call to create more effectively the possibilities of change.

The pseudo-liberal reactionary, on the other hand, has no sense of just proportions, because he has no human sensitivity to oppression. He finds no difficulty in parroting Billy Graham's talk about "We have all had our My Lais!" He doesn't think much can be done; it's always been this way, and time will cure all. He has no imagination for the plight or the desperation of the oppressed, because he cannot empathize with others outside his situation. He secretly prefers what he imagines to be the safety of the Establishment to the dangers of disruption, even while cultivating the prestige of talking as an "armchair revolutionary."

When the policeman's truncheon smashes the head of a dissenter, the pseudo-liberal reactionary sees only the angry word hurled by the ragged youth in the street, not the massive violence and unresponsiveness of the Establishment that has brought him to this point of frustration. So he secretly feels a self-justification at the sight of counter-violence directed against the dissenters. Tyranny, whose effects he imagines *he* can escape, bothers him less than disruption. As the struggle intensifies, the reactionary readily blames it on the minority of radicals who are visibly acting out their frustration in the streets, holds himself blameless thereby and justified in rejecting them, sides with the forces of oppression, and so helps to bring about a situation that will either explode in massive violence or create a reactionary regime.

The real blame for this reign of violence and reactionary repression must be placed on the shoulders of well-meaning but unresponsive liberals and liberals-turned-reactionaries, for they had some access to power and some understanding of the need for change and might have created the mediating forces. The radical, voicing and experiencing the need for change, has little access to power, and his ability to create mediating forces within the established society is very limited. If he speaks in an angry and confrontational way, it is largely to make up for his objective lack of decision-making power. However alienating his tone, he nevertheless speaks clearly enough that the liberal could well have understood his message if he had chosen to listen.

So it is essentially the failure of the liberal to respond that breaks the mediating bond between the two sides of the historical dialectic and creates reactionary repression. The radical is really the symptom of the disorder, not its cause, and is very seldom the one who can actually create change. To do so, he must either get into the present system of power or create an alternative one, and this choice immediately puts him into the same dilemma as the liberal.

The liberal needs the radical to deepen his consciousness, but the tide turns on whether he becomes massively involved or withdraws into inaction or reaction. The failure of the liberal is the real cause of polarization and reaction, and to blame the radicals for this is to mistake the toe that flashes pain for the body that is causing the pain.

The emergence of new creative forces hinges on the formation of a mediating group combining sensitivity to injustice, an access to power, and the political and organizational expertise to turn demands into realities. In short, the ability to create effective movements and parties of "radical-liberals" is the crucial test of whether or not a society is capable of creative change from within.

Radical-liberalism is simply a synthesis of the anger and hopes of the radical with the practicality and political understanding of a good organizer. Only this synthesis can bring together transcendent hopes and historical possibilities in such a way as to incarnate a new social order that can temporarily correct some of the evils of past situations. This cannot be done once-and-for-all, but only again and again in each new situation. And yet to do it at all in any particular situation demands that ability to "seize the time" which in ghetto language is called "getting it together."

NOTES

1. "French Intellectuals and Democrats and the Algerian Revolution," *Toward the African Revolution* (N.Y., Monthly Review Press, 1967), pp. 76-80.

2. Sam Brown, "The Politics of Peace," *The Washington Monthly* (August, 1970), pp. 24-25.

3. *The Washington Post* (Sept. 4, 1970), p. A7.

Chapter 12

Latin American Theology
of Liberation
and the Birth of
a Planetary Humanity

The theology of liberation today stands in a global context. It demands a stretching of the mind beyond the cultural frameworks of all previous human thinking to a new awareness of the universal *humanum,* which is, at the same time, an appreciativeness of the multiplicity of perspectives of the many peoples in their many situations *vis à vis* one another. We are called upon to experience what our people look like to the Vietnamese, to the Laotians and Cambodians, to Africans and Latin Americans. We are called upon to learn many languages and to take into our consciousnesses many histories to create for the first time a sense of the human which is beginning to transcend the ideological imperialism of one center and one people's aspiration that totalizes its power and perspective toward the world. It is a great, perhaps the ultimate experiment in human history, and so justifies a certain use of utopian and apocalyptic language.

For Christians, Latin America has a very special role in the development of a theology of revolution or a theology of liberation. It is in Latin America that the political theologies of hope, or liberation or of revolution, which European and American theologians, such as Jürgen Moltmann, or Harvey Cox have been developing, may take real root. To use the Marxist term, it is in Latin America that theologies of liberation in a Third World perspective may become more than armchair theory or a new kind of "missionary theology" (!) emanating from those who do not practice what they preach, and may become a theory that is created out of real *praxis*. For it is evident that for Latin America the theology of liberation has been *praxis* first of all. The theology of liberation is not a dogmatic *a priori,* but a creative reflection upon *praxis*.

For Christians, the contribution of Latin America is unique because it is the only region in the world where a predominately Christian people are aligned with the revolutionary developments of the Third World. The ambiguity and tragedy of Christianity are that it is a faith with roots in revolutionary messianic hope, which, nevertheless, was co-opted into the imperialist ideology and social structure of the later Roman empire. Consequently, a culture and a society originally antithetical to the messianic hope of Judaism, from whose loins Christianity sprung, became the historical vehicle of the Church, and Christianity itself was used to sanctify and perpetuate the hierarchical society and world view of classical culture. Yet, despite this Constantinian co-optation of the Church, Christianity nevertheless inserted into the stream of human history the seeds of dissolution of this hierarchical pattern of classical sacral societies. Its messianic impulse rose to the surface again and again in European history in a series of revolutionary upheavals which progressively shattered the classical ontocratic pattern of society and substituted instead a dynamic, historical view of human social existence, emancipated from static orders and open to the revolutionary demands of future hope.

Nevertheless, the integration of Christianity with imperial ideology and society had the effect of identifying Christianity with Greco-Roman and European imperialism in the minds of non-European peoples. As a result, the Christian faith has failed markedly to take root to any great extent in lands outside the original cultural basin of the Greco-Roman empire. Even the one important effort to extend Christianity into the Iranian world in Patristic times had finally to take the "heterodox" form of Nestorianism in order to disaffiliate itself from the "imperialist" Christianity of the Byzantine government. From the time of the breaking off of the African, Egyptian and Iranian areas of Christianity, first into heterodox and implicitly nationalist forms of Christianity in Donatism, Monophysitism and Nestorianism and then the falling away of these regions into Islam, peoples outside the Greco-Roman cultural basin have resisted inclusion into "catholic" Christianity as a religious form of the imperialist ideology of Western colonialism. Thus Constantinianism, which acted as the historical vehicle for Christianity in Western society, has also resulted in a decisive blunting of both the revolutionary "good news" and the universal humanity of the Christian faith. In the light of this fact, Christianity's claim to "catholicity" became as ideological as the claim of the Roman empire itself (from which this term was borrowed) to be truly "catholic."

Today this fact is of crucial importance for the consciousness of peoples of the historical Christian societies. A fundamental revolutionary struggle has erupted in the modern world that lies precisely between advanced technological countries of the West, who have exported their developmental advantage to the Third World in the form of colonialism and neo-colonialism, and those so-called "under-developed" countries, which are struggling to liberate both their bodies and their souls from this tutelage. This revolutionary struggle is both material and spiritual. Rather, we should say, it embraces the whole man, for national liberation and internal industrial development are now seen to hinge, not merely on developmental "seed money," especially when this comes from those countries which already hold these areas in neo-colonialist bondage, but rather on an inner revolution of spirit which liberates colonial people from the psychology of dependence and self-alienation and is based on a people's demand for its own integrity. A resurrection of the spirit of a people is the existential first fruits of liberation.

In Latin America this process of inner self-liberation is called *concientizacion.* Its theory and method have been developed by the exiled Brazilian educator Paulo Freire whose "pedagogy of the oppressed" is reflected in the theory and practice of liberation throughout Latin America. *Concientizacion,* in Freire's words, is "learning to perceive social, political and economic contradictions and to take action against the oppressive elements of reality." [1] Although Freire's method was a part of a literacy campaign, it is aimed not so much at getting people to "read," as at getting people to *see,* to articulate their situation. It aims at breaking through the pervasive "culture of silence," that defines the oppressed condition, by an inner resurrection of soul that transforms a person from an object of conditions which determine his reality and consciousness to a subject of his own history and destiny. Freire has harsh words about the doctrinaire leftist, as much as the doctrinaire rightist. Both demand a sectarian truth which they seek to establish by force, and each is threatened if "his" truth is questioned. Both demand infallible certainties and perceive doubt as a threatening rather than a liberating challenge. Freire's method, by contrast, calls for a self-opening to the truth, rather than the "bringing of the truth to the people," of Leninist elitism. The role of the revolutionary is to serve the people in a way that liberates him from elitism. He is to be liberated by the people as much as he is to liberate the people, by opening himself to the social truth revealed by their condition at the same time that he teaches them to articulate this social truth. The poor and the oppressed are the prophetic community, for it is in the contradictions of their condition that the contradictions of the whole society are revealed.

Freire's method is dialectical in nature. The dominant reality is a false reality that proclaims its right to dominate and define reality in the interests of its own power. But this ideological nature of its definition of reality is concealed by a pretense of standing for "being as such." Its concept of reality is static and totalitarian, and its methods of education are rote. The pedagogy of the oppressed, by contrast, is dialectical and iconoclastic. It is the teaching of "insight" into this ideological character of the "reality" of the dominant society and recognizing the false consciousness that supports the power structure. But this insight is an explosive, liberating force which breaks through the monolith of the dominant consciousness to stand over against it; to define oneself in opposition to it and to glimpse a new possibility beyond it. It is this rebirth which is the foundation of the "new man" who can create a new society. Freire's method would be called by many names in different movements for liberation. It would be called "Black Power" and "Black Pride" in the Black movement in the USA; or "consciousness raising" in the women's movement. It accords essentially with the psychology of liberation expounded in the context of the Algerian liberation movement by Frantz Fanon, in his *The Wretched of the Earth* [2] and Albert Memmi in *The Colonized and the Colonizer*.[3] It also corresponds to that dialectical consciousness which is at the heart of Marxist humanism.

In one of the last interviews before his death, the noted Marxist theorist György Lukács heatedly denied the false assumption that Marxism believes that being determines consciousness. For Marxism, that consciousness which is determined by the present form of society is precisely the false consciousness, the ideological consciousness. The revolutionary consciousness is that dialectical conciousness which breaks out beyond the present form of society, and the false consciousness that it creates, and perceives its ideological character. It is this critical consciousness, transcendent to social being, that is revolutionary consciousness, that enables the revolutionary to act upon social being to transform it. "Only in this way can we escape from the empirical weight of being." [4] For Lukács, the essence of Stalinism is its subversion of dialectical consciousness, and its definition of reality from the point of view of its own tactical opportunism. Thus Stalinism reasserts ideological consciousness within the *status quo* of a power structure called "socialist," and denies the possibility of further criticism. Because Stalinism everywhere dominates official Communist parties, Lukács denies that there exists anymore in this official communist ideology a genuinely Marxist method and theory.

It is in the sense of this kind of Marxist theory that Latin American theology of liberation sees its method as essentially Marxist. Thus it establishes a Marxist-Christian dialogue in the context of the concrete *praxis* of liberation, while, at the same time, having little use for the official Communist parties. But this critical consciousness it also sees as at one with the message of the Gospel which attacks the false power structure of the "Powers and Principalities," and which brings, through baptism, that inner revolution which brings to birth the "new Adam." Thus, for theology of liberation, the social content of the Christian doctrine of the "new Adam," reborn in Christ, is precisely the "new man" of Marxist dialectical consciousness which is brought to birth through *concientizacion*. But this critical consciousness also reveals the ideological character of the Church in Latin American society and thus sets the radical Christian as much against the ecclesiastical power structures, as it does against the generals and the bankers.

This perception of the ideological character of the Christian Church simply reaffirms that basic apostasy of Christianity which we have called "Constantinianism"; the suppression of the messianic dialectic of the Gospel and the ideological use of the messianic symbols of the Gospel to baptize the empire. Because the advanced technological nations of the world are "Christian" in this sense, the Third World historically has been the area that accurately perceived the true character of this "Christianity" as the ideology of European colonialism. In this way the fatal confusion between Christianity and its Constantinian vehicle was reinforced, making it all but impossible for the peoples of Asia, Africa, India and China to recognize, in the Christological idea, the impulse inherent in their own liberation struggles, or for most Christians to recognize the continuity of Christian faith with revolutionary hope. Latin America, as a Third World *Christian* region, then stands potentially as the key interpreter of the identity of Christian faith and revolutionary struggle.

Traditionally, Latin America has been a region subjected to the most rigid form of the Constantinian imperialist Church, as that was exported by a counter-reformation colonialist Spanish Catholicism. Yet, almost miraculously, its present revolutionary reality is creating a rediscovery of the messianic kernel of the Gospel within this gilded Constantinian encasement. Everywhere in Latin America today there are theologians, priests and laity, grasping with a remarkable clarity the messianic dynamic of Christian faith. This discovery pits the Latin American Church against its own inherited tradition and society in an agonizing way. Yet this struggle itself may be the crucial confrontation with that contradiction between messianic and Constantinian Christianity which has characterized Christian history. The Latin American Church discovers in its revolutionary need an explosively creative potential for uncovering that profound crisis with the Constantinian vehicle of the Church, which may also release, in a powerful and practical way, the revolutionary meaning of Christian faith as a gospel of universal historical salvation. Just as James Cone declares that it is only in the Black Church that the Gospel is truly proclaimed; and only the Black Church which can truly be the Church, so we might also say that it is only in Latin America that the real theology of liberation can be written, whereas Europeans and North Americans, who remain encompassed by their own status as beneficiaries of oppressive power, can only comment upon this theology from outside.[5]

The Golconda Movement in Colombia, which took up the challenge to build a revolutionary Christianity laid down by the assassinated Camilo Torres, reveals something of the practice of this theology of liberation. Unlike Camilo himself, the Golconda priests are essentially parish priests who work in the poorest *barrios* of the city. They thus respond to Freire's demand that the revolutionary go to the people and learn from the people, rather than imposing a theory and strategy from above. For them, theology itself is not a theoretical *a priori* of fixed doctrine, but corresponds precisely to that dialectical consciousness which must be discovered through action in behalf of liberation. Thus, according to René García, the leading spokesman of the Golconda group, even a theoretical Marxist Christianity "cannot respond to the revolution, for theology is done in action."[6]

The Golconda group used the Church's liturgy as the prime vehicle of *concientizacion*. It thereby recognized that, through its evangelization, the Church has instilled into the Colombian people a false consciousness, resigned to oppression and exploitation. It starts then with this very tool itself in order to revolutionize it and to create an evangelistic style in which "faith is presented as a factor of change directed toward a more just and human society." [7] The liturgical rites of the Church cease to draw people away from the real world toward a never-never land "above" or "beyond," and instead become a revolutionary celebration. "Participation in the liturgy demands fundamentally a community dedicated to social change and the building of a society where there is love and justice for all." The revolution of the Church's evangelical style must begin in the negation of its alliance with the corrupt and exploitative social system and end with the revolutionary thrust toward the "new man" of Marxism and Christianity. Such a revolution in the Church's practice demands a revolution in theology that totally overcomes the traditional antimonies of dualistic ontology and epistemology; that dualism of the spiritual and the temporal which has been the chief theoretical means of subverting the revolutionary content of Christian faith, and which is deeply rooted in the Latin American religious consciousness.

Faith must cease to be an intellectual affirmation about some "purely spiritual" matters, and must become incarnate in work and action; "every creative act thus becomes a protest against the established order." Other worldly hope is transformed into hope for liberation from oppressive and exploitative social and economic structures, and love is desentimentalized to become the functional solidarity of men and women struggling for a new and different future.

This destruction of the dualism between the temporal and the spiritual involves, for Golconda, a refounding of the theological enterprise. "From a theology of supernatural values superimposed on natural ones we shift to a theology in which the supernatural is integrated with the natural . . . from a theology which separates soul and body to a theology of integrated man; from an abstract to a political theology in which the people participate in the development of society in its economic, political and social areas."

The destruction of the traditional dualisms of classical

Christian theology demands a transformation of the semantic content of the religious symbols. Or rather, we should say, their ideological context is overthrown to reveal their true human content. Thus, for the Golconda group, the key Christian symbols of Incarnation, Revelation and Resurrection cease to point backward to some once and for all event in the past, which has been reified as a mysterious salvic power in the institutional Church, and becomes instead paradigms of the liberation which takes place in people here and now. Incarnation is not some mysterious metaphysical occurrence that defines the historical Jesus and is extended in the institutional Church. Rather "to be incarnate" means to be fully committed to the oppressed and to a political action which takes the anguish and hopes of the people seriously. Revelation is not some mysterious communication of supernatural truths which occurred only in Biblical times and has been frozen in the Church's teachings for all times. Rather revelation is that vision "which allows us to see political power as guardian and promoter of a system of privileges which the National Constitution was supposed to justify and which the Church sacralized." Revelation is *concientizacion*. Revelation is that redeeming and liberating insight which makes people aware of the social contradictions that define their lives, and thrusts them toward a process of liberation from dependency and oppression. Likewise, Resurrection is not an ancient miracle that applied only to Jesus, or perhaps to all men only after death and the end of the world. Rather, Resurrection is the sign of the "new man" who is being born in the commitment and struggle of making a new world. The Paschal mystery is that mystery of revolutionary suffering through which a new humanity and a new society are born. The Church itself as an institution must be fundamentally transformed through this struggle, so that it ceases to exist as a hierarchical structure set apart from the people and wedded to the old order, and instead becomes that "people of God" whose reason for existence is to be the servant and midwife of the process of liberation and the overthrow of the oppressive orders of society. The Church exists not for itself, but to serve the revolution.

Such a definition of theology and the task and nature of the

Church sets the revolutionary Christian fundamentally against the false consciousness and existence of the Constantinian Church, so much so that it should not surprise us that the Golconda priests, and those who represent their point of view in other Latin American countries, have been suspended by the Church and tortured and even killed by the governments. Yet so deep is the need for social change in Latin America that this new understanding penetrates quickly and deeply into the viewpoints of the younger priests and laity and even some of the bishops. At the Medellin conference in August of 1968, a moderate commitment to social change as the task of the Church was endorsed by the Latin American bishop's conference as a whole (CELAM).[8] Thus the Latin American Church stands as perhaps an example of the most radically polarized church in Christianity, spanning as it does, the most rigidly Constantinian and sacral view of the *status quo* of the old hierarchical society and the most radical revolutionary interpretation of the mission of the Church.

The polarization is radical and immediate especially because the Latin American Church must face directly the question of armed conflict, and the justification of armed conflict as the means of making the revolution. The example for the embrace of armed conflict has already been given by revolutionary priests, such as Camilo Torres in Colombia and Domingo Lain. Here the traditional Church is caught upon the horns of its own tradition which has always baptized the "just war" on the side of the powers that be, and so it has little resources with which to argue a theoretical absolute pacifism with revolutionary priests, who far more persuasively argue the need for a "just war" on the side of the revolution. For revolutionary priests, the necessity of armed conflict is not determined by the revolutionaries, but by the unjust violence of the *status quo* which maintains its own power by force. If the present power structure were actually open to persuasion and change by peaceful means, this would be far more preferable as the method of change. The violent explosion is always the most dangerous method of making change, both in its cost to the people and in its possibility of creating a fanaticism in the Left that will lead to a new ideologically dogmatic society. Yet the reality of the power structure is such that it cannot maintain itself except by force, a force increasingly shored up by counter-insurgency training and arms and even direct intervention from that North American power which benefits from the asymmetrical relationship between developed and "underdeveloped" areas. Since this power structure, with its North American support, will not change voluntarily and within, it can only be overthrown by force. The Christian justification for this is essentially the argument from the "lesser of evils"; the argument that the violence of the revolution is a lesser evil than the violence and injustice of the maintenance of the *status quo*. Those, such as Pope Paul VI, who decry violence as essentially un-Christian prove themselves unable to focus on the prior violence of the power structure. Violence is ascribed only to the revolutionaries, whereas the violence of the establishment is defined as "just authority." [9] Thus the deplorers of revolutionary violence reveal their essential self-identification with the present power structure and their self-encapsulation within its ideology. In the words of Camilo Torres:

> They have often told me that I preach violent revolution; but it is interesting to see why the ruling class portrays me as an advocate of violent revolution. You have realized that my proposals can be reduced to this; that the majority exercise power and that the government decisions be taken in favor of the majority rather than the minority. . . . The ruling class knows who will decide . . . whether the revolution is peaceful or violent. The decision is not in the hands of the lower class but in the hands of the ruling class. And since the lower class is beginning to organize itself courageously and with discipline and decision, and since we are not organizing for elections, they assume that we are organizing for violent revolution. This is why the minority ruling class intends to unleash violence against the majority class. . . . Those who choose violence are those who can afford it. [10]

Don Helder Camara, the bishop of Brazil who has for many years identified himself with the struggle of the oppressed, represents a mediating position in this struggle. Deeply impressed

by the philosophy and tactics of Dr. Martin Luther King, Helder
Camara rejects violence chiefly on strategic grounds. For him,
the violence of the ruling class and its North American sup-
porters is so harsh and terrible that any use of it by the revolutionaries will bring a blood bath far greater than the good
that the revolutionaries could hope to achieve. The revolutionaries must fight by alternative non-violent means, seeking
power by routes that do not entail armed conflict. In this way
the revolutionary process becomes also one that builds a community of reconciliation and love and avoids that paranoia and
mentality of reprisals and doctrinaire control on the Left characteristic of revolutionary societies established through armed
conflict.[11] There are few in Latin America who would disagree with Helder Camara about the theoretical preferability of
a revolution built in this way. The question remains, however,
not in the hands of the revolutionaries, but with the establishment whose violence prevents social change by other means.
With the increasing eagerness of the United States to add its
counter-revolutionary violence to that of the traditional oli-
garchies, whether change without armed struggle really remains
open as an option is thrown more deeply into question.[12]

Guerrilla warfare, as it was developed in China, and
adapted in Vietnam and Cuba by strategians such as General
Vo Nguyen Giap and Che Guevara, as well as theoreticians
such as Regis Debray,[13] is a method of armed conflict which is
adapted to the essential disparity of technological power between the developed Western powers, which hold Third World
peoples in thrall, and these peoples who seek to liberate themselves from colonial and neo-colonial power and to begin a
process of internal development based on autonomous self-
direction. The disparity of technological development means
that insurgent peoples cannot meet their masters on their own
ground. They cannot beat them with their own kind of technological weaponry. Rather, they must seek to go underneath and
around this kind of technological might, by building a solidarity
with the masses of the oppressed people which will subvert the
power structure from below. Where the power of the colonial
and neo-colonial occupying powers lies in brute force, the power

of the guerrilla lies in his ability to convince the people that he stands for and is identified with the injustice of their situation. Only within the framework of this identification between the guerrillas and the people can a guerrilla movement "work," for only then can the guerrillas fade in and out of the masses of the poor population in a way that makes them invisible to the pursuing armies. So far few guerrilla movements have succeeded in establishing this kind of solidarity in Latin America. Moreover, the counter-insurgency methods developed to defeat the guerrillas in South East Asia have been applied to Latin America to raise the price of such methods to an intolerable level. It is no accident that General Westmoreland himself was transferred from his role as leader of the American war in Vietnam to the Southern Command, based in Panama, which is the center for American counter-insurgency training for Latin America.

However, once a guerrilla movement establishes this kind of solidarity with the people, brute force reveals its essential impotence. A terrible calculus then arises in which those who would defeat the guerrilla movement must all but destroy the land and the people themselves in order to finally get at the invisible guerrillas who move among them. It is this terrible calculus which is revealing itself in its true genocidal proportions in the American war in Vietnam; which has made refugees of a third of the population and devastated large portions of the land surface beyond prospects for rehabilitation in the immediate future. The fact that the United States has been willing to go to such lengths to establish its ability to defeat a guerrilla movement, which has long been known to be no immediate threat to American security, raises questions about its purpose. There is no doubt that a part of this purpose was the insistence in the Pentagon of a need to "make an example" throughout the world of the determination of the American military to establish its will against such a movement and the inability of a guerrilla movement to win against American might. Latin America, undoubtedly, was one of the chief places that was to "take note" of this object lesson. Yet the enormous devastation that has become necessary in Vietnam, still without clearly establishing this "object lesson," may ultimately have the opposite effect. It may have the effect of discrediting the benign purposes of the United States throughout the world and establishing in the minds of all civilized people the fact that the price of defeating a genuinely popular struggle for national liberation is one that no decent people can be prepared to contemplate. If this "lesson" is learned by Americans in South East Asia, Latin Americans will undoubtedly be among the chief beneficiaries.

Christianity and Revolution

In Arend van Leeuven's provocative books *Christianity in World History, Prophecy in a Technocratic Era* and *Development through Revolution*,[14] this revolutionary struggle is seen as integral with the Christological mystery of human history. Christian society was a paradoxical fusion of the classical hierarchical world view of traditional sacral societies and the revolutionary dynamism of Hebrew messianism. The result has been that Christian society has continually experienced a tension and internal revolt which unleash this buried messianic dynamic against every effort to incorporate it into a static, ontocratic framework of a totalitarian society. From the conflicts between pope and emperor in the Middle Ages, to the explosion of the Reformation against the sanctified Church, to the explosions of modern revolutions in France, America and Russia against sacral societies, this messianic dynamic has continually surfaced, shattering the boundaries of every attempt to incarnate it in a fixed social structure.

For Van Leeuven, secularization is itself an expression of this messianic dynamic which revolts against the effort to incorporate messianic faith as the sanctification of a classical hierarchical society that is presumed to mirror a fixed cosmic order of heaven and earth. European Christian man was thus forced out of the shell of classical man and sent out on a revolutionary path in search of that "new creation" that shatters the boundaries of every static reality. Secularization represents the historical transcendence of messianic faith, which shatters the vertical integration of heaven and earth of the classical ontocratic pattern of society. Thus the messianic heart of Christianity erupts within Christian society itself in a dialectical relationship to its classical Constantinian historical vehicle.

In a similar way the Western revolutionary impulse spreads to the rest of mankind in a dialectical manner. The historical dynamic of advanced Western societies sets traditional societies in Latin America, Asia and Africa in an internal tension which ultimately works to dissolve their classical sacral orders and to substitute a revolutionary ethos. All societies around the world begin to experience a revolutionary momentum, in the form of a demand for the improvement of life. But these technological, secular and revolutionary styles of life, sparked by the impact of the West, are acted out in non-Western or non-developed societies only in an anti-Western or anti-imperialist revolt against colonial tutelage.

We can then, perhaps, begin to chart a movement of the whole globe toward a new unity through the spread of this pattern of revolutionary culture, but only through each cultural area and each people striving to realize this revolutionary possibility in the context of its own identity and integrity as a historical people. Development toward a new planetary humanity goes hand in hand with the revolt of every oppressed group, in demands for national, class, racial, and sexual integrity and identity. Men can move closer together only on the basis of each group's self-realization. The social revolutions which rock the modern world are perhaps the working out of this manifold revolutionary process. Communism and socialism have become the dominating ideologies of this self-realization because they too are secularized messianic ideologies which spring from Christianity, but in an anti-ecclesiastical, anti-sacral fashion. They incarnate the Western hope for revolutionary development, but situate themselves in an anti-imperialist relationship toward the institutions of Western society. Thus they allow non-Western peoples to catch the Western revolutionary fever, but in their own terms; i.e., through revolt against Western tutelage. The world is in a culminative crisis in which hopes for radical salvation mingle with images of total warfare and annihilation.

In this seemingly ultimate world adventure of mankind, the Biblical mythology of apocalypse and paradise come close as genuine, practical alternative. Mankind will either conquer necessity in a non-oppressive form, or else the revolutionary tension bred in mankind by its Jewish-Christian roots will end in a final explosion. Van Leeuven believes that, in this revolutionary situation, it is the responsibility of Christians especially to recognize the theological dimension of the liberation struggle, and to develop a theology of revolution that can guide and interpret it (and prevent Western powers from destroying humanity in an effort to prevent its birth!).

Such a theology of revolution must recognize the irreversibility of the revolutionary momentum. From the perspective of the eschatological mandate laid on human history by the Gospel, it is equally apostasy to identify Christianity with Constantinian Christendom (which the momentum of the Gospel has, in fact, already invalidated in Christian societies themselves), or to identify the messianic mandate with any future revolutionary society which might emerge on the other side of any social crisis (i.e., Stalinism or the imperialism of the Left). Messianism puts an end to any static societal integral of heaven and earth; society and its transcendent possibilities, and places heaven (transcendence) ahead of man as the source of constant exoduses to new possibilities. History is opened up as the arena of the infinite. To teach men to live humanly, repentantly and yet joyfully with this historical tension is the task of a Christian theology of revolution in that modern revolutionary world to which Christianity itself has given birth. In order to find a new human society which can live in this radically *historical* manner, man must do nothing less than give birth to a new humanity which can resist the age-old temptation to dogmatize and eternalize his human historical works and yet not make of the Revolution a Moloch which devours each present generation for the sake of that future "new man" who is never here, but always "on the way." Like the people of the Exodus we must learn to live by faith, gathering manna from day to day, pressing on to the Promised Land, neither hoarding yesterday's accomplishments, nor looking back to Egypt, nor yet becoming unable to rejoice in God's daily grace in the name of those future kingdoms which are not yet here. It is in Latin America where this conflict described by Van Leeuven, both in its ecclesial form, as the conflict between messianic faith and the Constantinian Church, and in its social-political form, as the conflict between the imperialist "Christian" West and the anti-colonialist liberation struggles of Third World peoples, meets in a crucial form.

Yet it seems that the last heresy that must be let go of is precisely that "Christocentrism" that presumes that all that is messianic and revolutionary can be mediated only by the historical Judaeo-Christian tradition. We must perhaps be willing finally to see that God is the God of all men and is revealing himself to all men in their histories. If Christianity is rediscovering a revolutionary human dynamic, as it moves from its classical framework into a new form which integrates transcendence with history, so too other classical faiths may be going through similar revolution that fits their classical religious symbols also to stand as symbols of human liberation. It should not surprise us that it is precisely in Vietnam where we find the ancient otherworldly religion of Buddhism (which, like classical Christianity, demeaned the reality of "this world" for a spiritual reality over against all that was *visible* and *bodily*) being reshaped by the revolutionary struggle so that its hope for salvation becomes a hope for human liberation that will rise out of the struggles of the Vietnamese people against the imperialisms of China, France and the United States.

In the book *We Promise One Another*,[15] a collection of poems from the Vietnamese liberation struggle, we find, as the concluding statement, the poem "Night of Prayer" which might be described as the poetry of a Buddhist "theology of liberation."

In that moment
wind was still

birds silent
seven times seven Earth shook
as Immortality traversed
the stream of Birth-and-Death
The Hand on the wheel
in the mudra of Peace
bloomed like a flower in the night.

That Moment
the flower of Immortality opened
in the garden of Birth-and-Death
The Enlightened smile;
word and symbol
He came
to learn Man's language.

That night in Tusita Heaven
doves looked down
saw Earth, my homeland, brighter than a star.
While galaxies inclined, worshipping
'til East turned rose
and the Lumbini gardens became a soft cradle
welcoming Buddha, newly born.

Tonight, tonight on Earth, my homeland
men look up
their tear-blind eyes turn toward Tusita Heaven.
The screams, the cries of pain are everywhere.
As Mara's hand bears down
Violence, Hate.

In Darkness Earth, my homeland, thirsts
yearns for the miraculous event
when Eternity parts its curtains
shadows dissolve
and the Long Hoa (the Buddhist Messiah)
    comes to my land
When the Sound of Being echoes again
in the singing of a child.

Tonight, the moon, the stars, bear witness
let my homeland, let Earth pray
for Viet Nam
Her deaths and fires
grief and blood . . .
that Viet Nam will rise and from her sufferings
become that new soft cradle

for the Buddha-to-Come
Let Earth, my country, pray
Once more the flower blooms.

Tonight we hope
our agony bears fruit
that Birth-and-Death will cross
the stream of Being
and Love's spring bathe ten thousand hearts,
that Man will learn the language of the Inexpressible
and the prattle of a child
will teach the law.

NOTES

1. Paulo Freire, *The Pedagogy of the Oppressed* (N.Y.: Herder and Herder, 1970).

2. Frantz Fanon, *The Wretched of the Earth* (N.Y.: Grove, 1963); *Black Skins: White Masks* (N.Y.: Grove, 1967).

3. Albert Memmi, *The Colonizer and the Colonized* (Boston: Beacon, 1965).

4. "Conversation with György Lukács," by Franco Ferrarotti, *World View*, Vol. 15, no. 5 (May, 1972), pp. 30-35.

5. Perhaps the leading theologian of Latin America at the present time is Gustavo Gutierrez. His *Liberación, opción de la Iglesia Latinoamericano en la Década del 70* (Bogotá: Presencia, 1970) is being translated for Orbis Press.

6. René García Lizarralde, "Habla Golconda: Toda la Iglesia en la Revolución?" in *Núcleo* (Bogotá), no. 37, Sept. 12, 1969, p. 4.

7. *Ibid.*, René García. All the quotes from the Golconda Group are from "Religion in the Revolution: A Look at Golconda," *NACLA Newsletter*, vol. 3, no. 10 (Feb., 1970), pp. 8-10.

8. See *Between Honesty and Hope: Documents from and about the Church in Latin America* (Maryknoll: Maryknoll Documentation Series, 1970).

9. François Houtart and André Rousseau, *The Church and Revolution* (New York: Orbis, 1971), pp. 215-216.

10. From the Speech to the Labor Unions, printed in *Vanguardia Sindical* (Bogotá), July 23, 1965; reprinted in *Revolutionary Priest; The Complete Writings and Messages of Camilo Torres*, ed. and intro. by John Gerassi (N.Y.: Vintage, 1971), pp. 260-261. For a general introduction to the life and thought of

Camilo Torres, see Germain Guzman, *Camilo Torres* (N.Y.: Sheed and Ward, 1969).

11. Dom Helder Camara, *The Church and Colonialism; The Betrayal of Latin America* (Dimension, 1968); see also José de Broucker, *Helder Camara; The Violence of a Peace Maker* (Dimension, 1969).

12. For some of the recent thinking on Christianity and revolutionary violence, see Luis Carlos Bernal, *La Violencia; plantiamiento moral del problemá en America Latina;* faculty of Theology; University of Louvain (1970); and Robert Bosc, *La Violencia y la no violencia en el pensamiento de la Iglesia,* (Buenos Aires, 1968), IDOC #68/112. Cited in Houtart and Rousseau, *op. cit.,* pp. 222-23.

13. Samuel B. Griffith, *Mao Tse-tung on Guerrilla Warfare* (N.Y.: Praeger, 1961); Vo Nguyên Giap, *People's War; People's Army: Viet Cong Insurrection Manual for Underdeveloped Countries* (N.Y.: Praeger, 1962); Che Guevara, *Guerrilla Warfare* (N.Y.: Vintage, 1961); Regis Debray, *Revolution in the Revolution: Armed Struggle and Political Struggle in Latin America* (N.Y.: Grove, 1967).

14. All three of these volumes have been published in English by Scribners, in 1964, 1968 and 1969, respectively.

15. Edited by Don Luce, and published by the Indochina Mobile Education Project (Washington, D.C., 1971), pp. 115-117.